Tatiana Chemi

The Art of Arts Integration

Theoretical Perspectives and Practical Guidelines

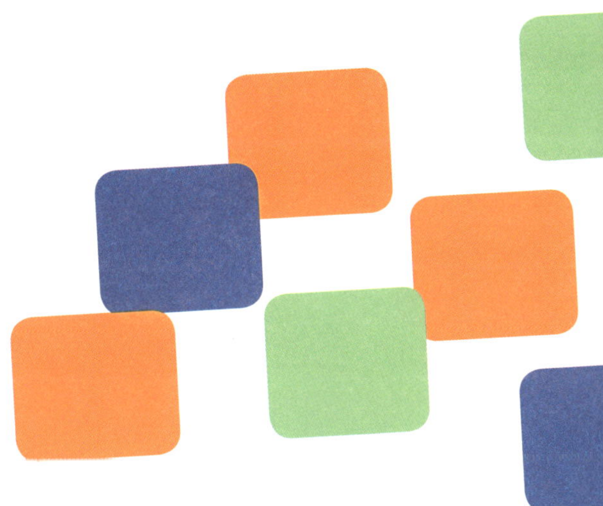

AALBORG UNIVERSITY PRESS

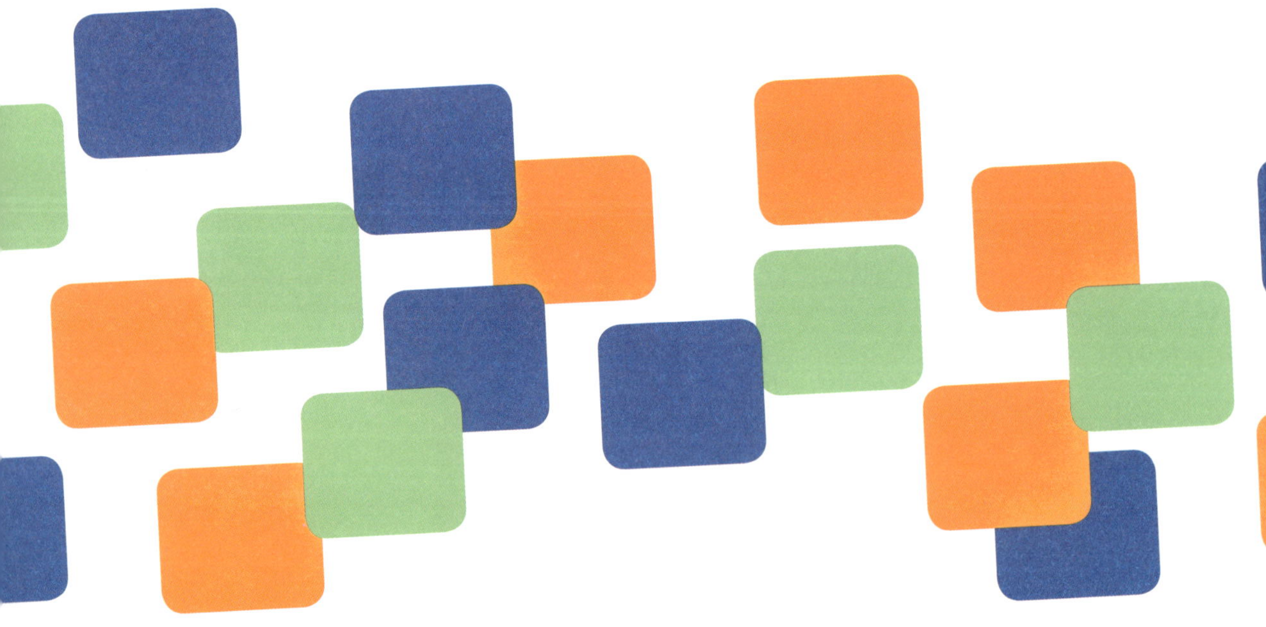

Questo libro è dedicato a
mia madre e mio padre,
i primi educatori
che mi hanno introdotto
alle pratiche di Montessori
e che hanno stimolato e incoraggiato
in ogni modo la mia voglia di sapere.

This book is dedicated to
my mother and father,
the first educators
who introduced me to the Montessori method
and who have enouraged
and supported my drive
towards learning in so many ways.

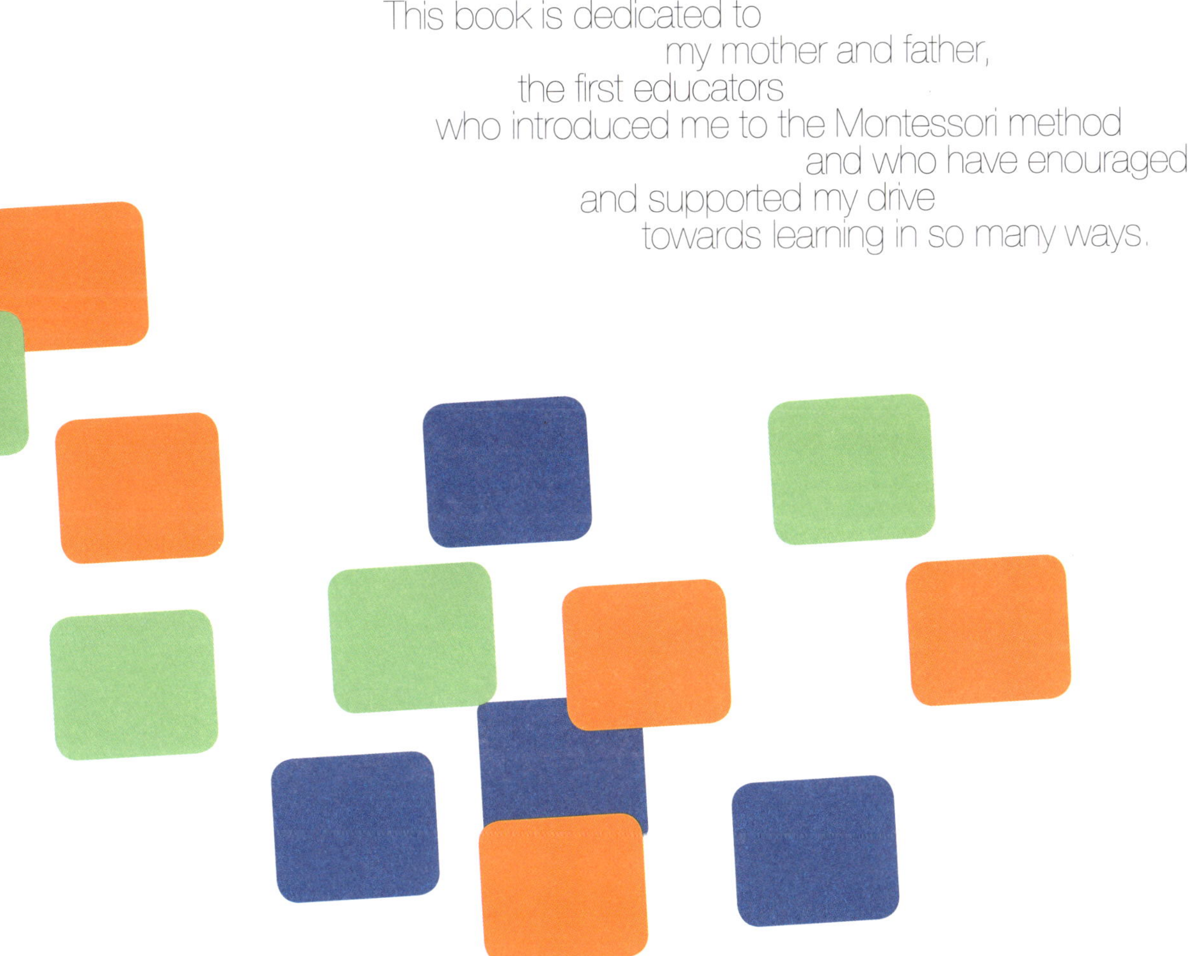

List of illustrations

Contents

Foreword

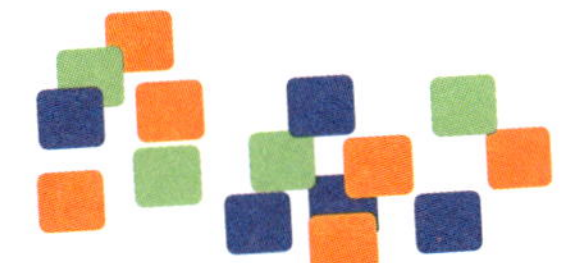

By Shari Tishman

I remember the first time, many years ago, when I saw the slogan, *Art is Good*. The scene was a crowded city bus, and it was printed on a button pinned to a young man's jacket. I was in college at the time, and I believed – as many young students do – that deep ideas were complicated and esoteric, to be found by laboriously making one's way through dense texts and endless conversations. So I was stunned by incredible directness of the button. How immediately and effortlessly *true* it seemed. Yes, I thought, that's it exactly: Art *is* good. Good to make, good to look at, good to experience. But even as I savored the apparent simplicity of the slogan, I couldn't help thinking about the complex questions it raised. *Art is Good*. Good for what? Good for whom, and in what ways? Good like vitamins? Good like pleasure? Oh, and what kind of art? All art? Who decides? And so on.

This is a book about arts integration. Its purpose isn't to offer answers to all of art's big questions, but it does stake out a compelling territory: The arts, Tatiana Chemi argues, are good—*profoundly* good–for learning and teaching. This view, of course, is no less complex than the statement, *Art is Good*; and the author does justice to its complexity. She argues for an arts-centric approach to pedagogy, and introduces the concept of Artfulness, which she defines as an artistic way of thinking about learning that bridges the cognitive and emotional dimensions of arts-based learning, and brings together thinking and making. Arts integration, on Chemi's view, is not just a way of giving students more art into school, but rather a way to support creativity and innovation across all school subjects.

Many years after I first saw the *Art is Good* slogan, I had the good fortune to work on a research initiative called *Qualities of Quality: Understanding Excellence in Arts Education*. My colleagues and I at Project Zero at Harvard Graduate School of Education conducted scores of interviews and site visits in order to understand how experts in the field – administrators as well as educators – conceived of arts education's best purposes and characteristics. Our findings align beautifully with the ideas and practices written about in this book. For example, if you ask art educators what arts education is good *for*, they'll likely mention a multiplicity of purposes, including (but not limited to): developing young people's capacity to think creatively, to make connections, to reflect on big ideas, to encourage self-exploration and self-expression – all things that Chemi discusses. If you ask arts educators what signs of excellence they look for in the actual practice of arts education – in other words, what they see "in the room" that tells them that quality learning and teaching is going on – they'll likely mention many of the characteristics that Chemi explains and celebrates: Exploration and experimentation, curiosity, a rhythm of reflection and making, engagement, emotional openness and honesty, high focus, a sense of purpose, a sense of joy.

These characteristics are dear to Chemi's heart. Building on the concept of Artfulness, and through many compelling practical example, she argues that arts-centered learning experiences, at their best, bring together cognitive intensity, joy, a sense of challenge, and a sense of purposeful engagement – for teachers as well as students.

Works of art are more than the sum of their parts, and they often have multiple entry points. The same is true of this book. Composed with a sense of artfulness, the book is divided into three sections that speak to three big questions about arts integration: How can we make sense of it? How do we achieve it? How can we evaluate it? These questions are discussed through the lens of the author's own research as well as through her extensive knowledge of theory and practice in the field. But while the book is well-grounded in contemporary scholarship, the reader is never far from a vivid classroom example that brings into focus the real experiences of students and teachers. Just as the author argues for the power of art to stimulate curiosity and create engagement, the many real-life practices artfully woven into the text are sure to engage and entice a wide array of readers. It's a pleasure to think about the power of this book to help educators bring the power of art to learners everywhere.

Shari Tishman,
Cambridge, USA, 2014

Shari Tishman

Shari Tishman is a Senior Research Associate at Harvard Project Zero, and a Lecturer at Harvard Graduate School of Education. Her research focuses on the development of thinking and understanding, learning in museums, and learning in and through the arts.

Foreword

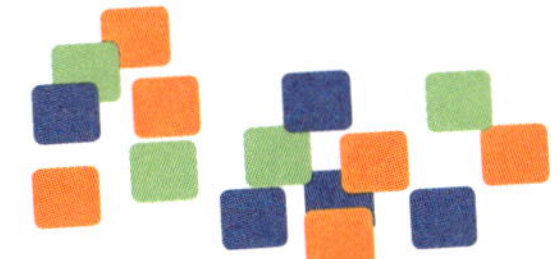

To the original 2012 Danish version

By Jørgen Lyhne

Dear Reader,

The textbook that you now hold in your hands is very unusual and it deserves a very special kind of attention from you. If you realise this, you have now the opportunity - so to speak - to meet the book on its own terms.

Look intensely at the book. Feel it in your hands. Consider the weight of it, the paper's texture. Lift the book. Lower the book. As if you need to feel its exact weight. Feel now the surface, the cover, the back, the sides, the pages.

Breathe in deeply and take in the scent of the book. Which fragrance did you register? You can put the book up to your ear and listen to it. If you scratch a little on the book's surface, you will hear a specific sound. If you open the book and leaf through its pages, you will hear it whisper.

Our senses are with us all of the time. We are surrounded by sensation. Our senses connect us with the physical world. Not just the world that is around us, but also the inner world. The senses tie it all together in the body and knowledge.

Sense is the basic condition for the higher mental functions: reflection and cognition. Along with aesthetics and the taste for the beautiful form, perception is the background for cognition and learning.

This book highlights that there are multiple pathways to learning and development. While we obviously cannot disclaim the need to maintain knowledge and reflection as an important basis for development and learning, there is another way. The way in which creativity, aesthetics and perception are the main source of learning and development.

Tatiana Chemi argues in the book that society's demands for increasing the creative capital of the labour market and in society as a whole should lead the school system to develop methods and forms of learning that will enhance the students' creative learning. She demonstrates that schools have a need to experiment with creative teaching methods. She provides inspiration for the development of teaching methods and materials. The book is evidence-based and builds a bridge between theory and practice.

The publication provides both a compelling argument for the ideas regarding arts-based education, and gives practical inspiration and suggestions for teachers.

In addition to the reliable use of international and national research in the specialised topic "art-based learning", the book involves the author's experience and insight into learning research.

So, dear reader, you're sitting right now with a book in your hands, which collects and disseminates valuable experience from a problem area that few researchers in Denmark have looked at.

Read on and be challenged by the author and let her guide you along new paths which will invite and inspire you to contribute to the development of Danish education.

Enjoy.
Jørgen Lyhne, 2012

Jørgen Lyhne

Jørgen Lyhne is Associate Professor at VIA University College, where he teaches in special education and psychology at the Undergraduate School of Education. His teaching areas include:

- Cognition and neuropsychology
- Positive psychology and positive education
- Psychology of learning processes
- Flow and meaningfulness
- Social emotional and existential intelligence
- Music psychology and education

He is an author and executive editor of the psychological-pedagogical journal Cognition & Education, published by the Danish Psychological Publishers.

Acknowledgments

I wish to thank the Department of Learning and Philosophy for the financial support for this book project and all of my colleagues for the inspiration and support that makes my work more joyful and interesting. Due acknowledgments go to: All of the teachers, pupils, school leaders, museum coordinators, artists who contributed to this study with their knowledge, experiences and excitement, Jørgen Lyhne, who has reviewed the Danish version of this book and has written a Foreword to the 2012 Danish version, Mark Gallacher for his language support, Howard Gardner, Shari Tishman, Ellen Winner, Steve Seidel and all their colleagues at Project Zero, for showing the way in the field of arts integration and for their good advice, Marianne Bager for allowing me to use her model in Figure 15, Peter Kastberg for his collaboration in the field of Science Theatre and last but not least, my lovely family and my friends all over the world.

More information

Glossary

More inspiration

Exercises

Introduction

Learning
Is what happens to you
While you are busy having fun
learning

Tatiana Chemi

In 2012, when I was preparing my introduction to the volume that lays the background for this present one, I envisioned different ways of approaching education and a picture of a little girl emerged. At that time, I imagined that this little girl, like millions of others, went to school. In the morning she would get up, eat breakfast and get ready. She would comb her long hair, brush her teeth and put on her pink dress and flat shoes. Then she would say goodbye to her parents and her younger brother and walk to school.

Her name was Fila and she lived in Afghanistan. The little school that the village had courageously started, consisted of no more than a tent in the desert. There were only a few chairs and tables, so most of the children had to sit on the floor. When the wind blew it covered the children's books with a fine dust of dark yellow desert sand, and blown sand would sting their eyes. Nevertheless, the kids from the village rushed to school every day. Boys and girls courageously resisted –and still resist- the Taliban version of Sharia, which prohibits a common education for both sexes and strictly excludes girls from any form of education or public employment.

Fila was a fictive character, born from my imagination, but she seemed as real as any child I knew and her motivation to go to school was not so different from my son's motivation: the desire to learn and to develop and understand the world. My motivation for wanting an education for my son corresponds to Fila's parents' wish that she can learn something she can use in the future, to watch her develop and see her understanding of the world around her grow. However, the significance of Fila's school attendance reaches well beyond Fila's life: every step she takes towards the school is a step she takes for the sake of humanity and our hope for an equitable and democratic future.

Am I exaggerating? If I just think of how brave Fila is, I believe that the above is a quite realistic view. In the meantime, after the book was published, a real Fila shocked the Western media with her story: Malala Yousafzai, an 11-year-old girl from the little town of Mingora in Pakistan, was recruited for a school blog project. Strongly supported by her father and hated by the Talibans, she was shot but miraculously, survived. Her blog and persistence made her a role model for child and youth activism, standing for the democratic right to education (Rahman, 2014; Yousafzai & Lamb, 2013). In my envisioning, Fila was frightened, Malala too. Fila wanted to attend school, but she was afraid of being killed by a bomb and she was afraid that the Taliban would return and punish her or her family for her natural desire to learn, Malala told of her fears in her blog, her book and the many interviews that followed. The two girls' fear has no comparison with my son's fear of being teased at school. The probability of his school being hit by a bomb is infinitesimal. His is a world where he's more at risk from obesity than anything else. The contexts in which these children learn and develop are vastly different, but their learning experiences are as rewarding and energising. All children, regardless of age, gender, geographical and social background, whether they are well functioning or mentally disabled, thrive under the same conditions for well-being, and learn if they thrive.

Research on the preconditions for optimal learning clearly shows what kids - and individuals more generally need. At the same time, statistics (e.g., Education for All, 2011) show that the world is far from experiencing a fair level of democratisation for learning and education. The challenges that Fila and Fila's teachers face are very different from the ones my son and my son's teachers struggle with.

Aware of the above - that while school contexts can be diverse, teachers and pupils develop under the influence of the same basic positive terms – I wish to address the present book to a certain type of school, where educators believe in a progressive way of thinking about learning and training, in schools that wish to meet the challenges of creative efforts and innovation. Perhaps such a school is a privileged environment: Basic needs are met, no child is starved, abused or threatened by war, where it is possible to focus beyond basic needs, to explore creativity and self-realisation. In our present society and in the case of any society that is not affected by famine, war and lack of basic human rights, it is possible to apply a flipped version of Maslow's need-pyramid (Maslow, 1943), where basic needs are not only physiological but psychological. The basic needs for the future are intangible: Security, social relations, creativity, self-realisation. The challenges that our society is experiencing, make creativity and job satisfaction basic needs that we cannot ignore.

This book is aimed primarily at the creative school and its brave defenders in a joint effort to continue to further develop the well-functioning elements and find new creative ways to meet our children's needs for learning, development, confidence and positivity.

The background for the book's perspective on good teaching is a specific theoretical tradition and a specific research and development project. The theoretical framework is presented in the chapter "Theoretical perspectives", which focuses on concepts such as Progressive

Education, positive psychology and cognitivist understanding in an easily accessible manner. The specific research framework is supported by the ambitious Danish project MMALP – "Mange Måder at Lære På" (Many Ways of Learning).

The MMALP project started in 2008 and was part of a larger research effort initiated by Vejle Municipality in the central part of Jutland, Denmark. The purpose was to give the entire school system an opportunity for research-based development and to contribute to the debate on engaging learning and teaching forms with development-based research. The project had a duration of less than three years (2008-2011), and it involved all of the schools in the municipality, a total of 35 schools with 1,600 teachers and 12,000 pupils. All of the players in the Vejle municipal school system were involved in both quantitative (job satisfaction surveys and statistics) and qualitative research (case-based stories on specific development projects).

Seeking to contribute to a broader and more nuanced understanding of the many ways education and learning can be provided in primary schools, MMALP coordinated many different voices. One of these voices has been Artfulness research, which has documented what happens in schools, and how schools create and support good learning and teaching with specific focus on artistic, aesthetic and creative learning and teaching methods.

Besides using MMALP for field observation and inspiration, I have used other shorter qualitative studies on art in education in this book. The result provides both a practical handbook for practical application in the classroom and a theoretical perspective on the integration of arts in teaching: Part One: "How can we make sense of it?".

In Part Two: "How do we achieve it?", I look at the practicable aspects, tools and exercises, and suggestions for teaching are described. I am deeply grateful to all of the teachers and educators who allowed me to observe and interview them in research projects, which I used in writing part two. This book could not have been written without them, their courage in embarking on new innovations and their willingness to contribute to the documentation of their work. Some practical materials in this book are a true account of teachers' experiments in the classroom, others are based on my observations and are further developed accordingly. The exercises are explained step by step and supplemented with short meta-reflections and comments.

In Part Three: "How can we evaluate it?", I provide some convenient tools for self exploration. The tools are qualitative and described in a simple manner so that teachers and educators can find practical inspiration for qualitative evaluations. The alternative may be an alliance between the school and scholars, in this case, the book offers the tools to understand the qualitative researchers' work and logic. This can make the future (re)search alliances easier to establish and to understand.

The purpose of this book is to inspire the teachers who believe that creativity should be a central focus in school, and that artistic creativity can greatly contribute to a more creative and reflective school. This inspiration is offered in the form of accounts of the significant benefits that the integration of arts in teaching offers, such as positive emotions and cognitive intensity, but also in terms of concrete, effective practical tools.

These practical tools must not be read and construed as strict rules or instructions, but viewed and used as inspiration and encouragement, where the educator takes individual elements and transfers them into their own educational context. In essence, I suggest the reader views these materials as recipes for creative teaching. As we use them in the Italian cooking tradition: as an Italian I was raised with the utmost respect for the family cooking tradition. When an Italian is old enough, he/she (normally a she) gets assigned to the family's treasured recipes. What all take for granted are the measures. All dimensions and quantities will be equal to the size of one's mother's fist. It is up to the individual child to estimate the amount that is neither expressed in kilograms or pounds. Sugar and flour are weighed by the eye, and the baking point is checked with the sense of smell. In the same way, the recipes I suggest in the present book should be smelled and touched within a specific contexts. My biggest wish is that my readers will find their own quantities, their unique size that can be used in their creative cuisine. When this size is finally found, I wish to encourage those readers who would like to experiment with artistic creativity to pick elements, concepts, understandings and approaches from this book and apply it to their own unique context. With their own mother's fist.

In other words, the practical exercises are an invitation to the artistic tradition: Not a "push" but a "pull" towards learning, experience and reflection. An invitation to dare to break new ground and to let themselves be charmed and seduced by the world of art. My purpose is to help teachers to see specific opportunities for a practical application of art forms, products and processes in education, and their possible integration with other school subjects.

There are many intelligent methods or tools that can make a difference in the individual's learning and self-development. Some educators advocate mindfulness, concentration and presence; others differentiation (learning styles), quality (Harvard Project Zero, for example), optimal experiences (flow). There are also educators who focus on curiosity or positive experiences. With this book, my intention is not to advocate any specific tools as the best tools for learning, but to describe the artistic learning processes as unique and rich learning opportunities that can create good quality in learning. Art is a flexible and safe playground for learning, but learning outcomes often depend - here and in the other methods – on many different and concurring elements, on context and quality. Attention to quality is what can make art, mindfulness, flow, learning styles, etc., flourish for the benefit of an optimal learning environment and experience. Art can contribute with its inherent attention to quality, shapes and professional pride.

Although literature on learning and creativity shows that there are many methods that work in the classroom, this book will focus on the artistic way to stimulate learning and creativity. The reader is invited into and guided through the artistic playground. It is important to clarify that creativity and innovation are not positive phenomena as such. The positive side of the creative and innovative skills is what we choose to do when we create. Sometimes, the creative process is neither positive nor negative, a creative process, for example, which is based on and stimulates democratic values, tolerance and openness can never come up with new, creative and innovative deadly weapon. This book focuses on the artistic methods because I believe that this field offers virtually untapped learning potential in educational and teaching practices.

This book is primarily written for teachers and educators in elementary school, but school boards and parents can also find inspiration and tools. Last but not least, this book can inspire school management to think creatively and encourage their employees to focus systematically and consistently on creativity. Together with schools, I also address artists from all arts forms, cultural entrepreneurs, museums, science parks and libraries that have focus on learning.

A final conceptual note should address my use of the word "art". The subject of the book's narrative is actually a grammatical plural: different art forms and school development projects, involving different types of art in many ways. These arts all contribute to an understanding of the integration of the arts in education, by means of the elements they have in common in learning contexts. Therefore, when I talk about art, I refer to the various arts, and the concept should be understood in its plural form. Specifically, this book looks at several visual arts such as design, painting, animation, architecture, drama and theatre. I also examine arts-rich learning environments: Expeditionary Learning, which uses an expedition-based curriculum in schools, integrating art forms with all of the school subjects; mindfulness in education as the sensory contribution to students' resilience; a specific form of dramaturgical experience that integrates natural sciences with performance and museums as optimal learning environments.

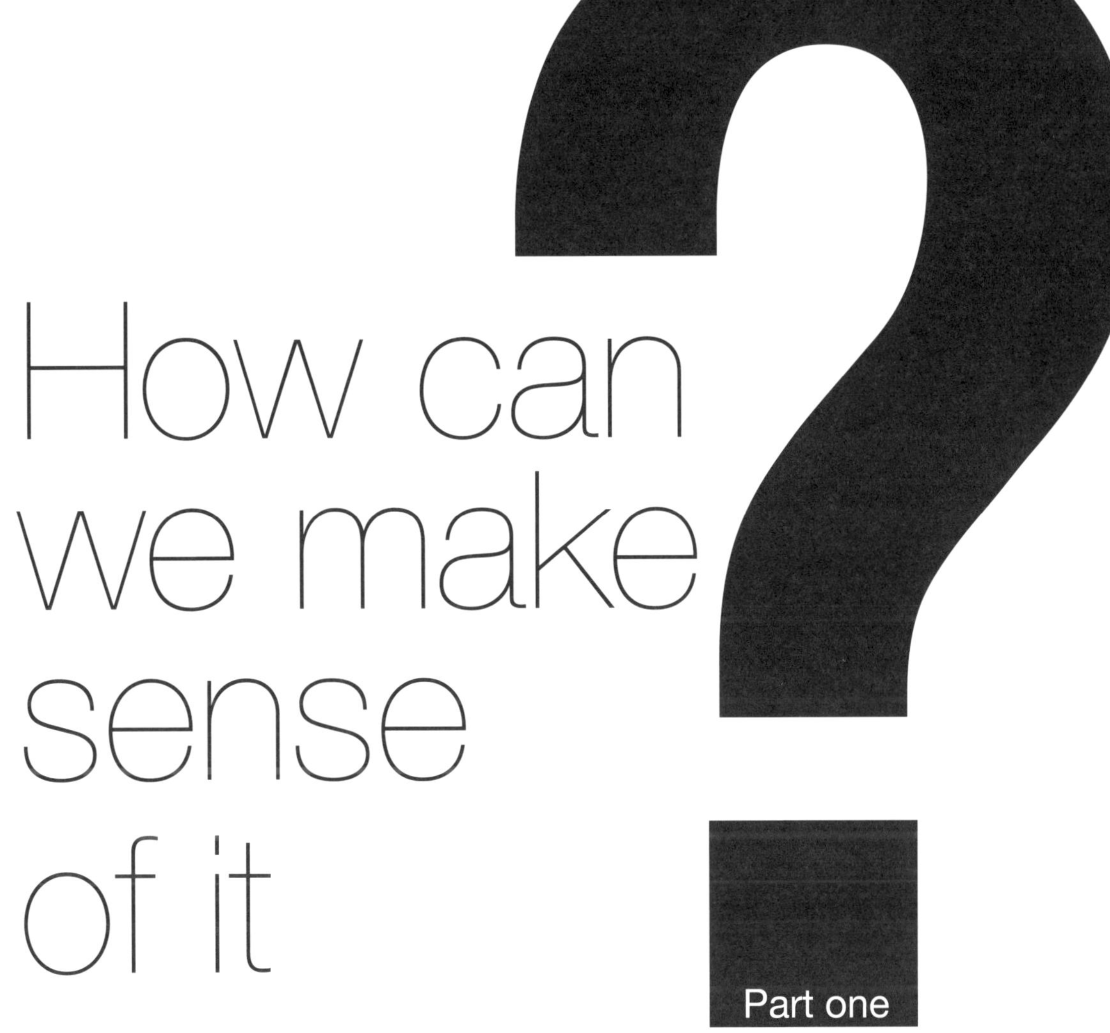
How can
we make
sense
of it
Part one

The creative effort

During the Many Ways of Learning project, almost 2,000 practitioners working in the school system in Vejle Municipality in Denmark, were asked to evaluate their own and their pupils' creativity. The majority of the respondents ranked their own creativity as being higher than their pupils' creativity. On what basis? And what importance do the teachers ascribe to this visible gap? Can anything be done about it?

The questionnaire addressed the subject of creativity in the following first person point of view positive statements, which the teachers and educators had to read and then indicated to what degree they agreed or disagreed with each statement (Knoop et al., 2011):

My pupils are good at tackling academic challenges that require new thinking
My pupils are good at tackling personal challenges that require new thinking
My pupils are good at tackling social challenges that require new thinking
My pupils are sufficiently realistic
My pupils are good at setting themselves inspirational goals during lessons
My pupils are good at pursuing their own inspirational goals for lessons
My pupils endeavour to create something original in the lessons
My pupils support each other in being original during the lessons

I am good at tackling academic challenges that require new thinking
I am good at tackling personal challenges that require new thinking
I am good at tackling social challenges that require new thinking
I am sufficiently realistic
I am good at setting myself inspirational goals during the work
I am good at pursuing my own inspirational goals during the work
I endeavour to create something original during the work
I encourage my pupils to create something original during the work

The responses from these categories have caused researchers to puzzle over the visible gaps within the subject of creativity in schools. When schools place special focus on creativity and innovation as the driving forces behind the area of learning, how is it that the teachers cannot register measurable results in the pupils' creative development? What goes wrong? Where does the link between the stated strategies or between the visions and the creative practice break down? What significance will we ascribe to this gap in understanding?

Playing the devil's advocate, we may well ask: If the teachers are so creative, why do they fail to inspire the pupils with their creativity? What answer can we find and what can support the decision-makers and politicians in relation to schools when they (and they will) initiate some visionary project called "creativity in schools" or "creative children"?

The first step may be to acknowledge that articulated gap and take a closer look at what the teachers and educators at the schools are experiencing. The second step could be the separation of teachers' and pupils' creativity: Teaching creatively and boosting the pupil's creativity are two very different phenomena, which require specific strategies (Starko, 2001). A closer observation of the creative processes in the classroom and in the staffroom may provide a more precise picture of what is going on.

On a societal level, if we put the teachers' view into perspective, the basis for this gap in creativity may reflect the paradox that the creative subjects in schools find themselves at the centre of: On the one hand, society is faced with the demand to be creative, but on the other hand, state schools are struggling to systematically integrate creativity in learning and teaching. Pundits and practitioners everywhere identify creativity as the key competency in the future (European Union, 2009) and maintain that it should be implemented as a core initiative in the future. The media no longer talk about a trend, they talk about a necessity: We have to be more creative in the future if we are to survive. We have to be more creative so we can compete with the Asian tiger economies and to find sustainable solutions that preserve the natural resources we exploit so industriously. To introduce children to creativity is necessary for their future and for everyone else's future – a future where information flows at ever faster speeds and changes requires a new cognitive approach.

But even though creativity is contemporary society's – almost biological – necessity, school systems around the world are faltering in their attempts to implement a radical integration of creativity in teaching and learning. It does not look as though society's requirements can be met by the schools' ability to work with creativity. Despite radical changes in our contemporary world, such as globalisation, technology, increasing complexity and speed "we insist on educating our children as if all these things are not happening" (Robinson, 2011). This is reminiscent of Ron Ritchhart's complaint about American schools' failed attention to thinking: "failing at smart" (Ritchhart, 2002, pp. 3-11). He claims that despite the many attempts with focus on the nuanced ways of thinking ("deep thinking"), schools still experience fiasco. "Although Karen mentions understanding, thinking, reflection, and metacognition (thinking about thinking) as important, students never engage in these practices in a way that imbues them with any meaning" (Ritchhart, 2002, p. 5). Similarly, the above results from MMALP can be interpreted this way: Even though teachers and educators name creativity and innovation as an important part of learning and development, it seems that pupils are not engaged in creativity practices in a way that is meaningful to them. Just as Ritchhart asks "How could we fail at smart?", we can ask "How could we fail at creative?"

Ritchhart's answer is based on an analysis of the American school system, whose daily routines are not all that different from its European or Scandinavian counterparts. In the USA, schools continue in a tradition that values results, abilities and standardised measurable tests, even though their vision is to cultivate a more progressive approach to learning. Clearly, this gap exists because the schools have not incorporated the creative vision: The progressive approach remains limited and localised, without any hope of changing school culture as a whole. "The overriding message is this: Do the work, get the grade, and move on" (Ritchhart, 2002, p. 6). A similar situation is evident in Vejle Municipality in Denmark, where art in teaching is seen as a kind of fancy topping, in contrast to real bread-and-butter education. For example, in the research project Artfulness, some teachers had integrated animation with Danish and mathematics lessons (Chemi, 2010a). They named several dilemmas, one of these being the objective of the lessons. They articulated the schism between academic and creative subjects by separating three different forms of learning: 1) Learning in its broader understanding, as a (self) development process, and applied learning, 2) Academic learning, aimed at professional competency; 3) Learning focused on national tests. There was an implicit frustration in the fact that specific results were expected in the national tests, which takes time away from experimental and creative teaching and learning. If the pupils are expected to achieve a high PISA score (Programme for International Student Assessment hosted by the Organisation for Economic Co-operation and Development - OECD), the lessons would have to focus learning towards abilities and competencies within measurable parameters – in other words, the teachers will have to teach the pupils the best way to carry out the PISA tasks. Learning is thus interpreted as being directly proportional to a high score, and the children will acquire learning by rote, which they will quickly forget as they go on to get more useful competencies.

This approach differs from an educational design that is focused on academic learning, where the pupils can acquire specific competencies but exclusively in the areas that the Danish Ministry of Education has determined as having value. The teachers separate the two above-named approaches from learning as a whole, where creativity and an experimental approach have a good chance of developing. Based on my case study with these teachers, my impression is that the schools would like to give more space to forms of creative teaching and learning but they have very little time and they are under a lot of pressure to deliver good PISA results. The consequence is creativity projects that are small and limited in scope, which do not spread to the rest of the school or to other schools. In other words, the practitioner cannot establish – or help to establish – a school structure based on creativity. As creativity expert Ken Robinson, writes: "Occasional courses in creative thinking have limited value. Like rain-dancing, they underestimate the nature of the problems they are trying to solve" (2001, p. 3). Small and limited projects that as a whole only pay lip service to creativity will not cause the revolution that the schools need or want.

Let us examine this paradoxical development in the Danish state school system, where the tendency is to strip time, resources and attention away from creativity, creative approaches and experimental initiatives. The Danish state school system is measured and rated by PISA results and no longer by the children's development and general process of forming. The creative subjects are cut back and struggle to survive even though they are constantly being reminded by the decision-makers about their importance: See for example, Anne Bamford's "advocation" (2006) for the academic output within the creative subjects – arguments, which are popular among teachers in the practical music subject but which are dismissed by researchers (see for example, Journal of Aesthetic Education, 2000).

To sum up which attention points that the schools should clarify if or before they will work with creativity or promote creativity among their pupils and staff, I would point out the following: Clarification of the school's real need or engagement in the integration of creativity in the classroom; elucidation of creativity terms and the teachers' own understanding of the terms; establishment of an ambitious strategy, which extends beyond the individual process in the classroom; facilitating and rewarding creative strategies.

More concretely, the schools can use the following reflection guide as a way of getting a creative strategy started.

Reflection Guide for teachers, kindergarten teachers and school leaders

Aim: To prepare a system perspective for creative strategies in the school.

When: When the school will devise a creative strategy or determine clarification regarding creativity as a theme.

Practical proposal: To structure and design the dialogic reflection using a specific and meaningful involvement in creative initiatives or experiences (see for example, the artistic narrative text box).

COMPREHENSION PHASE

- What is creativity in literature? What does creativity mean to me as a practitioner? What does creativity mean to us as a school?
- Why is creativity necessary?
- What does promoting, implementing and cultivating creativity involve?
- What limits do we have to overcome as practitioners in schools?

Artistic narrative

Used as a different kind of kick-start for creative reflections and brainstorming.

- The participants bring different photographs, postcards, pictures (the more ambiguous the better).
- The material is put into a pile and each participant takes one item.
- The participants organise themselves into pairs or small groups and tell a story around the item that they have chosen.
  - If the picture was the beginning of a story, what would the story be?
  - If the picture was taken in the middle of an event, what would the story be?
  - If the picture was the ending of a story, what would the story be?

Other sources on creativity and learning as inspiration
www.creativityatwork.com/featured-creativity-innovation-articles/

SYSTEM IMPLEMENTATION

- Where do I find my creative inspiration?
- What sources of creativity can be used in the school?
- How do we envisage a school that is based on creative learning?
- How do we specifically implement the often chaotic creative processes in the school?

FACILITATING AND REWARDING

- Who can help me/us in this process?
- Where do we find the know-how, partners and help that can support a creative process?

Creativity is a strange phenomenon: everyone wants it and wants to implement it but only a few dare to do it. For good reasons. The creative processes are often chaotic and rebellious, particularly in some phases of the process. It is important that the school considers how it will integrate the creative chaos in a school system that is very structured. Especially when schools choose to integrate artistic creativity in the classroom. This type of creativity requires time and space to develop, because as some teachers in Vejle say, "art is a detour", i.e. a longer path towards learning (Chemi, 2010a, p. 41). This detour is time-consuming because it takes longer to reach the destination and it consumes a lot of mental energy, in that several faculties have to be engaged in the effort to reach the goal. As one teacher in the case study's animation workshop says, "I think, we have to get from A to B but we can still take a detour. But regardless of the goal or requirement we set, we have to get through ... we have to get over there somehow. Well, that's how I see it anyway" (ibid.). This important perception of art as a non-linear process should be discussed and looked at before the artistic process or strategy is started in the school. A lack of clarification can create unnecessary frustration and resistance to the creative vision. What should be discussed is

ART/ANIMATION AS DETOUR

Lone: Because it doesn't do anything, it's a detour.

Dorit: And there's a real curve that you don't notice all that much.

(Chemi, 2010a, p. 40)

whether the artistic experiences in learning are a worthwhile use of our time and resources.

These reflections should be supplemented with an overall clarification of the school's learning ideals. If the school's ideals are to meet standards and achieve satisfactory PISA results, then the Ministry of Education's learning goals and guidelines are probably the best strategy. But making teaching standards, PISA results and textbooks the goals of education, is the equivalent of claiming that the goal of driving a car is to complete a specific route by driving perfectly nicely and by sticking exactly to the speed limits (Ritchhart, 2002, p. 8). Teaching and learning need more than that. Especially if the school's ideal is a type of learning that is creative, motivating, inspiring and useful. In this case, the school must consider how standards and the creative strategy can come together. "Unlike standards, ideals can't be tested. We can't check them off or set a threshold of performance that must be met. However, ideals can do something that standards cannot: they can motivate, inspire, and direct our work" (Ritchhart, 2002, p. 9).

In this effort to be creative, art and the artistic processes contribute a great deal to supporting an optimal change. This book will show how artistic creativity can make a difference in new teaching initiatives.

Artfulness: An artistic way of thinking about learning

What is Artfulness

When I began some years ago to reflect upon the aesthetic learning processes and the scope of art's influence on learning, I quickly encountered a conceptual issue: The lack of a concept or a language that could communicate the diversity within the field. My understanding of the implications between art and learning, among other things, has been guided by a framework called *Artful Thinking* (Tishman & Palmer, 2006). Research into *Artful Thinking* focuses on how the individuals think when they are stimulated by works of arts or artefacts. However, my assumption was that reflection and thought were only a part of the experience, where creation is equally important and as rich in learning. So my focus area included both *the thinking* and *the making*.

At the same time, my previous work with *Expressive Arts* (Knill, Levine & Levine, 2005) strengthened a more nuanced use of art in contexts which were not traditionally artistic, such as art used in therapy, healthcare areas, coaching, meetings facilitations and in organisational learning (see for example, Austin & Devin, 2003; Chemi, 2006; Darsø, 2004; King & Vickery, 2013; Taylor, 2012).

My intention was to look at the intersection of three areas where art and learning are related differently. These pillars are well known as the following learning elements:

- Learning inherent in professional artistic processes (the professional artist's field).
- Learning that occurs when the art is transferred to non-artistic contexts using processes based on art or artistic processes (e.g. art in coaching or teaching in schools).
- Learning that can occur when using art as a metaphor, i.e. to think or learn "as if" one were an artist (for more about the metaphor's effect, see for example, Winner, 1982, pp. 252-264).

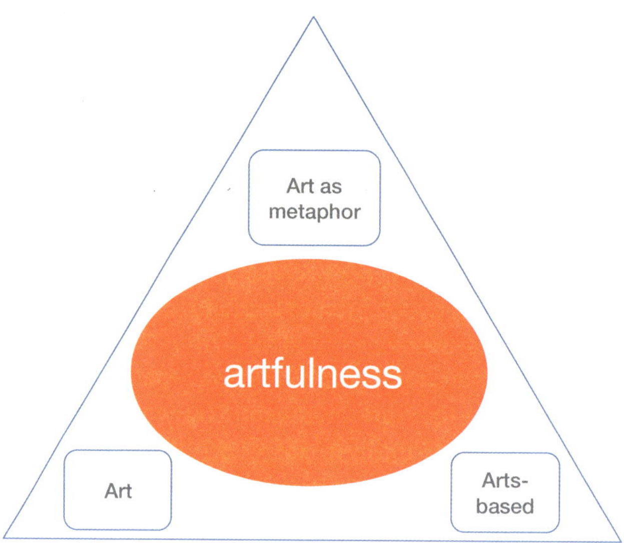

Figure 1 Artfulness triangle

As the above figure shows, I define this intersection as Artfulness. Artfulness is my definition and is a term describing a cognitive and emotional response to stimuli, which the individuals experience within the artistic or art-based experience. The difference between the three pillars within Artfulness (Figure 1) can best be understood in comparison to related terms: Aesthetic, art-based and artistic.

1. Aesthetic: Anything to do with the enjoyment of beauty - a sensory awareness. For example, a forest walk, meditation or culinary experience.

2. Art-based: Anything based on a practical experience of art and its processes but not necessarily created by professional artists. This is to do with "the making", the creation of artworks or artefacts and a personal engagement in the artistic processes, which do not necessarily take place in artistic contexts.

3. Artistic: Anything relating to art, when art is executed and perceived either as professional (in the case of professional artists) or art-specific (in the case of amateurs).

4. Artful: When art and its processes are used as a metaphor for something else. It is important in this perspective to emphasise that a given phenomenon can for example, be seen or interpreted as if it were an artistic endeavour or activity. For example, when the conductor metaphor is used to describe a leadership role.

According to Webster (1989, p. 84) "artful" in English characterises something that is "done with or characterised by art or skill". But the English word can also have a negative meaning, as in "artificial", "cheat" or "sly" and "cunning": See for instance Dickens' Artful Dodger in *Oliver Twist*. This is why I prefer the term "Artfulness" rather than "artful", because it is reminiscent of the term *mindfulness*, which is a heartfelt state that I believe should be a fundamental element of good learning environments (see also Ritchhart & Perkins, 2000 and Langer, 1993; 1997; 2005).

Artfulness is a term that, based on the aesthetic learning processes, means to think and act as an artist. For example, Artfulness is used when individuals are creative and innovative. An artful approach to learning and teaching can also be seen as an expression of a specific type of creativity: The holistic creativity, which merges logic and feelings, rationality and body. This term has been dear to Dewey when he studied what we can learn from art and artists (Dewey, 2005). The current study takes its point of departure from Dewey's area of interest and understanding for learning as experiential and experience-based.

According to Jackson, Dewey maintains that "[works of art] hint at what life might be like if we sought more often to shape ordinary experience in an artistic manner. [...] They thus offer indirect lessons about fashioning the more mundane aspects of our lives" (Jackson, 1998, p. 6).

Theoretically, you can see Artfulness as an intersection of the individual's perspective (the green areas in the flower model - Figure 2) and a societal perspective (dark blue areas), where the individual's greatest experience is a flow-like state of cognitive challenges and positive emotions. At a societal level, Artfulness can be said to utilise specific artistic elements and functions: To be productive and to create and communicate, and at the same time use different materials, media and strategies for the purpose of expressing, communicating, provoking, creating, etc. Keeping to this same theoretical approach, we can define the social relationships (the pale blue areas) both as the cultural "glue" that makes it possible for Artfulness to occur, and as a potential output of an artful process. The social relationships are both the foundation for and a consequence of an artful process.

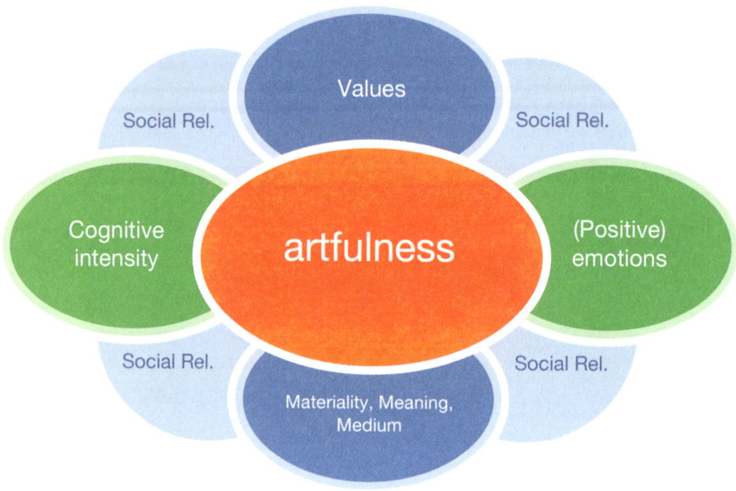

Figure 2 The flower model: Artfulness as crossroad

What is special in Artfulness is that the artistic experiences are not just seen as passive entertainment but as an excellent opportunity to think deeply, both in terms of reflecting upon works of art or artistic processes and in the analysis of artistic actions. A visitor to an art museum who looks at a painting for a couple of seconds and says he likes or does not like the picture is not using artful thinking or behaviour. On the contrary, a visitor to an art gallery who enjoys the details of the painting, who questions and ponders over the work, compares it with other works or his own life, etc., is taking a deeper approach to art, to thought and to life in general. Or a person who is actively involved in drama, is able to develop special competencies when this activity gets "under the skin". If this happens, then behaviour has changed, which in this case is characterised as "artfulness", an artistic metaphorical quality. My premise is that individuals can be trained in Artfulness, and by training they will stimulate a special disposition for deep thought.

During my study and collaboration with the schools in Vejle in Denmark (Chemi, 2011), I have paid attention to all of the three pillars within Artfulness and have chosen to focus on the green line in the Artfulness flower model: The individual level, where positive emotions and cognitive intensity are in balance. The Artfulness study, which is the research basis behind this book, focuses therefore on art or art teaching, but also observes the wider cultural approach to the process of creative learning and development.

Artfulness is not:

- A method, but it is a research field that invites teachers to cooperate and explore together.
- A medicine, but it is an approach that makes learning whole by reintegrating all of the elements of teaching in their wholeness.
- A recipe that everyone has to follow, but it is one of the possible ways of integrating wholeness in teaching.
- Teacher training, but it is rather an opportunity to implement good practice and reflect upon what works, what does not work, why it works and how educators can repeat this in a constantly changing world (Chemi, 2010d).

Artfulness in school

When I started my Artfulness study, my premise was that including art in teaching could help the pupils to learn. Despite the many different types of learning that the teachers and pupils experienced and reported on, the results have shown that none of them described "deep thinking" or deep and nuanced reflection, i.e. what I had defined as cognitive intensity. Unfortunately, the link between the practical creative activity and the more reflective part, which is inherent in the artistic processes, was in effect absent from the observed art projects.

Because of this, the pupils' encounter with art and the artists has basically been more about an approach to craftsmanship. The special time frames in the different projects were flexible and spacious enough to give the pupils a different learning experience. An experience that is inspired by the way the artists think and create and the way the artistic processes are put together. Furthermore, all of the development projects in the Artfulness study have been particularly characterised by a collaboration between a professional artist: An architect, a painter, an animator or teachers, which the pupils experience as amateur artists and experts in the arts.

This encounter with art, based on first-hand experience, gave the children many positive experiences, several specific tools and a surprising and rewarding learning output. But it is a far cry from what the teachers at a focus group interview qualified as typical for forms of learning for arts: Joint learning, both for the teachers and pupils, which opens up diverse points of view, appreciation and abilities to be attentive and open. Teachers thus define what is typical for the aesthetic learning processes: "What lies in the aesthetic processes is the reflection, together with the pupils: You offer views, opinions within, by recognising them and listening to them" (Chemi, 2011, p. 70).

Something I have not heard in the pupils' interviews in the Artfulness project, is an understanding for the aesthetic elements in works of art (e.g. form, colour, function, material) or a broader approach to art (artefacts and processes) from a historical or theoretical art perspective. Neither are the many opinions and approaches named, apart from the pupils at Andkær School, who believe that art's *relativity* is one of the biggest learning elements, which they take home with them from the project. These pupils have actually learned to decode the dynamic relationship between the artistic, formal and expressive quality: "[I've learned that] art doesn't always have to be exact and precise, it can be very different", "I've learned that you mustn't stop because the picture stops, it should look like it goes on. Just because the picture stops, the drawing doesn't", "It doesn't have to be precise and stop when it stops" (Chemi, 2010b, p. 51). They specifically know that artistic quality requires ways of understanding other than quality, e.g. in schools. In art, splashes on paintings can be regarded as learning opportunities or expressive elements rather than terrible mistakes. "[When] we sat down and made a blotch, it was just *so-what*," and not because cheating was OK but because the paintings "became prettier anyway". Of course the children know that they need to make an effort and should not paint outside the picture's borders but "if it goes outside the borders, it's still 'it'll be all right'" (ibid.) and not because within the art there is an expectation about *good enough* quality but because the judgement criteria in art is something else. What makes a work of art good is its formal qualities and the context of its use. The children at Andkær School learned this through a completely specific experience. They know for example, that what makes their paintings good is their visual qualities - the shapes and joyous colours and impressive sizes, but they also know that the context, where the paintings will be displayed (the underpasses at the school), makes a difference in how others respond to the paintings. They sound very precisely conscious of the diversity of responses to the works "when you drive the car [in the underpass where the pictures will be displayed], I don't think you see all of the details, so I think you just notice the colours and stuff" (ibid.). Or someone else will drive by not even noticing the pictures:

> Boy 1: For example, just by the Brejning viaduct, at the traffic lights, I think they just think: Yeah, fine. We want to get on. Let it go to green. And so I think they've different opinions, depending on who's driving past there.
> Girl, Boy 2: Yes.
> Boy 2: No, I think so too.
> Girl: It's – I mean I think a lot of people will think it was nice and: Hello! Who made that? and ...
> Boy 2: I bet they spent a long time on it or ...
> Girl, Boy 2: Yes.
> Boy 1: But I bet you there's also some people who won't pay much attention to it. (Unpublished interviews, Andkær School, 2010)

The pupils demonstrate a fairly good understanding of the artistic mindset despite the fact that the connection between the practical work and the work with the colouring book and a more thoughtful and theoretical dimension was not integrated during the course of the project.

For what concerns creativity and innovation, I also noticed that often the pupils in the art projects are not introduced to works of art or artistic processes as a way of thinking about new thinking or as training in innovation. This happens even in development projects that explicitly wish to link a research-based understanding of creativity to the practical artistic experiences and activities. The only exception within the Artfulness study that I can name, is the KDH (art, design, crafts) course at Engum School (Chemi, 2009b), which was initiated on the basis of a decision to teach the children innovation. However, this aim did not completely match the creative or innovative results for the way that the pupils created or thought. The pupils were introduced to brainstorming techniques and challenged to think "creatively" but they were not given any more guidance than that during the process.

This shows that even though the artistic processes rest on creativity and new thinking, it is not enough to establish a project using art to form creative children. Their encounter with art should be clarified, facilitated, put into perspective and guided, ideally by including professionals artists as inspiration and role models. As stated earlier, creativity or learning don't happen magically or automatically. The pupils may be unsure about what they have learned and experienced if they do not get the opportunity to reflect, metareflect and verbalise their emotional, sensory and intuitive learning.

To apply the concept of Artfulness in schools will to a greater degree, mean that the link between theory and practice should be implemented beforehand via a structured reflection – ideally, documented via log books, videos or research notes.

Reflection Guide for teachers, kindergarten teachers and school leaders

Theme: An artful school culture

Objective: To prepare a systematic approach to artful strategies at school (to think, learn, act as artists).

When: Whenever the school will prepare a creative strategy based on art or to achieve a clarification of artistic creativity as a theme.

Practical proposal: To structure and design the dialogic reflection using a specific and meaningful involvement of professional artists and the local community.

COMPREHENSION PHASE

- What does Artfulness mean to me as a practitioner? What does Artfulness mean to us as a school?
- Is art in school necessary for us? Why?
- What does promoting, implementing and cultivating artistic creativity involve?
- If we are to cultivate an artful approach, what limits do we have to overcome as practitioners in schools?

SYSTEM IMPLEMENTATION

- Where do I find my artistic inspiration?
- Which artistic sources can/should be used in school?
- How do we envisage a school that is based on artistic processes?
- How do we specifically implement the often chaotic and sensory processes in the school?

FACILITATING AND REWARDING

- Who can help me/us in this process?
- Where do we find the know-how, partners and help that can support a creative process?

Professional artists: Where do we find them?

In my work with art in organisational learning or at schools, I have often met many interested practitioners who express their frustration over the difficulty in finding artists who are willing to collaborate in specific development projects. Unfortunately, there is no specific catalogue or database that holds this information. But there are many ways to go about it that can make the process easier. Here are some tips:

- Visit your network in the local area: Art or culture associations, venues, galleries and talk with parents at the school.
- Ideally, visit major cultural institutions. If the project is innovative and ambitious, it will attract everyone.
- Ask your municipality about any art projects that involve for example, an artist in residence, or art clubs and associations.
- Visit art academies, acting schools, design schools, schools of architecture, film schools, animation schools, dance schools, etc. The young artists and art students are very engaged and will often gladly get involved in an important collaboration. This can even be a part of a school project for them.
- Art Festivals are an excellent occasion for meeting professional artists, especially if the event is based on reflection and the encounter between artists and teachers.
- Visit experts, gallery owners, museum managers, researchers in art and learning, seminars, etc. Everyone will be happy to share their expertise and a short telephone conversation costs little and can yield much.
- Professional booking agencies or event organisers have useful databases, especially for performing artists (musicians, actors, dancers, etc.) but will require a payment, unless the school makes a special partnership agreement. Worth checking out.
- Social media networks can be surprisingly effective: Write a message on Facebook, LinkedIn or on your municipality's electronic noticeboard.
- Projects funded by the European Commission are often keen to offer experimental collaborations.
- The Teaching Artist Journal (http://teachingartistjournal.wordpress.com) offers knowledge, inspiration and practical ideas.
- International networks can help. See for instance USSEA in the US (http://ussea.net) and InSEA in Europe (http://www.insea.europe.ufg.ac.at/index2.htm).

NB: It does not have to cost much or even anything at all. The reaching out phase requires a little preliminary work but once contact has been established, the project can offer the chance for sustained and long-lasting collaboration. The most difficult contact is the very first time you make an approach. But once professional artists or art experts see how much the collaboration has to offer, they will come back and they will spread the word among their colleagues. If the school can motivate these experts with an educational and rewarding experience, the financial benefits will become secondary – even if still important considerations.

In the Artfulness study, to my surprise, I identified a cultural gap between the artists and the schools. An artist or a teacher is like other professional individuals, a person who has specific academic values, understanding, artefacts and surroundings (Schein, 1992). The interviewed teachers and educators revealed that they think about art and learning in a different way compared to their collaborative partners in the arts.

The clear difference in the way teachers and artists express themselves can be seen in the model that I developed from my observations at Nørup School (Chemi, 2010a, p. 46) – shown below. The summary of the thoughts and opinions expressed by the teachers and artists in the interviews, clearly showed that the two groups think differently, are concerned about different things and attach different emphases to the themes they have chosen. To make this trend even clearer, I have counted statements within specific categories and noted the relevance and the length of each statement. Each statement is scored and evaluated in relation to the relevance of the category's theme and the length of the statement. Both relevance and length are tagged respectively with one point. That is, the columns in the table summarise how many statements the respondents gave about the given subject (one point per statement), the length (one point for a long statement) and the relevance of the statement (one point if the statement was strongly emphasised as relevant in the interview). The results in graphical form represent the answers from both groups (teachers are blue columns, artists are red columns) and in 16 different categories:

Academic (learning), learning (in general), cognitive intensity, flow, development, detour, help, what is special in animation, dilemma, *dropouts*, positive emotions, reflection, collaboration, self-expression, aesthetic criteria and observation.

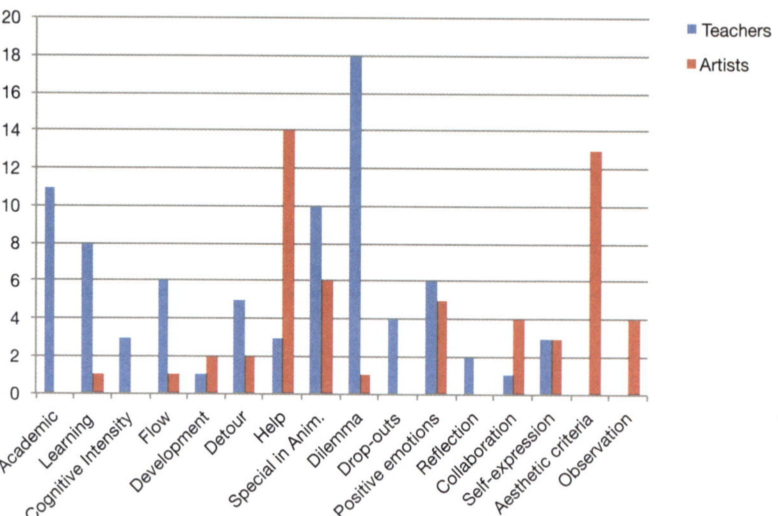

Figure 3 Teachers' and artists' answers, Nørup School

At first glance, we can see what occupies the teachers the most: not surprisingly it is the categories within learning or related fields such as academic learning, cognitive intensity, reflection and *dropouts*. This last category is related to the children who are struggling with general learning and who demonstrate that they really thrive in projects like the Animation Workshop. The latter is unsurprising: To be able to assess a child's development in such a short space of time (only a few days of teaching, a project week) then the teacher must have known the child for a longer period and it is understandable in this context that the artists do not comment this topic. They simply cannot know enough about pupils to have any opinion whether the pupils are improving their concentration on tasks or participation in the classroom. On the contrary, the teachers have often focused on the emotional consequences of the lesson for the "weak children" (according to the teachers' own definition) or *dropouts*, i.e. pupils who drop out of class lessons. Nevertheless, even though the artist does not expect any special focus on learning, it is significant that some categories within educational topics are not even named by the artists.

Similarly, the absence of any comments from the teachers related to the categories that are specific for the artistic processes and aesthetic criteria and the observation, is noteworthy. The observation, is defined here as a special artistic ability to observe visual and emotional details. The probable causes of this uneven distribution of statements and attention to the different categories is discussed below.

It is also significant, that the respondents ignore the process of development or Bildung, which is often related to the aesthetic or artistic learning processes both in literature (see for example, Catterall, 2009) or among the practitioners.[1] The teachers name "development" without providing further definition and the artists refer to a change, which can be interpreted as development but the major topics related to the process of Bildung are disregarded.

But what does this cultural gap look like at the schools in the Artfulness project? What are the basic elements in this encounter? Which themes, principles or practices are involved or in focus?

The model shown below provides a summary of the cultural difference within selected topics or subjects. In graphical and summary form, we can see the artists' mindset compared to the teachers' mindset: Their opinions, feelings or actions with certain art-related topics are expressed via key words or condensed sentences.

In consideration of the cultural gap, the most interesting projects are those that integrate a professional artist in the collaboration, which in this study is represented by Nørup and Andkær Schools' course with Hanne Pedersen and Erik Peitersen, respectively.

1 See for example, the teachers and educators attitudes in the focus group interviews, which were carried out in the Artfulness study.

Subject	Mindset	
	Artists	**Teachers/educators**
Artistic processes	"Studio" It takes time (to "digest")	The children's expression No waste of time (optimisation)
Artworks (product)	Creative associations The artwork's expression	The children's free expression The pupils' own expression
Artistic supplies	"Real" painting	"Real" painting is a surprise!
Specific objective	Public exhibition	Inside the school
Learning objective	Artistic "drive" Aesthetic and mediated output	To learn something (skills) Cognitive and academic output
Learning process	"Depth"	"Length"
Quality	Many ways to create	Details or acceptance?
Planning	"One day at a time"	"What will happen tomorrow?"
Main focus	Focus on the artwork	To complete a syllabus

Peitersen's vision of the art process was already formed from as early as the planning stage, which was contrary to the educators' wishes. Peitersen sees the artistic process as a professional artist and finds a solution that complies with his artistic mindset: A Renaissance-style studio. The course was designed as a common project that had a common goal, where everyone – pupils, teachers, artists and non-artists contributed with their abilities. The process was strengthened academically by the master artist (*maestro*) and the product can be said to be a joint artwork. This way of working was typical of arts studios in Italy during the late Middle Ages and Renaissance Period. Giotto, Michelangelo and other Old Masters, often functioned as master artists for a small group of apprentices who had to carry out the "mundane" tasks associated with the major paintings (often frescos). Peitersen created a similar studio at Andkær School, where the school functioned as a reservoir of apprentices with apprentice functions. The pupils took care of the "mundane" tasks rather than the innovative artistic process; they developed their abilities to create and express themselves within the very tight constraints. This set-up contrasted strongly with the normal way of teaching and learning in school, where the focus is on the educational output and on the pupils.

On the contrary, Peitersen paid no attention to learning or to the educational output. His focus was on the artwork and its internal rules and procedures. He designs and supports the process for the benefit of the end product. The choices he makes he makes in the service of the artwork. Does the artwork 'fit' the school's culture and surroundings? Does the artwork express the village atmosphere and closeness to nature that the school experiences every day? Does the final solution using the artwork's exhibition in the town work (for example the size of the artwork in relation to the underpasses)? How does the artist ensure the final qualify when amateur "apprentices" must execute the work? His solutions take place in the artistic world, where the artistic object must be shaped according to the artist's vision, idea, project, intuition or ideals.

Just like the artists in the Animation Project at Nørup School, Peitersen interprets his task as a team project, where he guides, inspires and plays with his apprentices. He demonstrates how the pupils can solve the practical tasks, he uses the language of the artist, he helps the children to point out mistakes and areas that can be developed and he values the children's efforts, perseverance and contribution.

However, this Renaissance-Studio perspective has been difficult for the coordination group. At the end of the interview, the coordination group was still frustrated over the original cultural gap:

> Educator 1: Peitersen was the one who said it had to be fine and attractive. […] Where we were more […] towards the other side.
> Educator 2: Yes.
> Educator 1: ... and said that well it was the kids, they were the ones who had to do it, and it had to be how they wanted it.
> Educator 2: And it's their intuition.
> Educator 1: Yes.
> Educator 2: And we're responsible for ensuring there is a lesson. (Chemi, 2010b, p. 66-67)

The coordination group in the Andkær project, views the educational or learning output as being the opposite to this controlled experience and does not see that the control has a completely different character because it is based in inherent artistic criteria. For example, Peitersen chooses the artwork's theme and develops the artistic form via a number of creative associations around the school's name. Rather than painting lots of ducks [Andkær School → Danish "and" = duck], it should be something round [Andkær School → Danish "kær" = pond, a little almost round body of water] and resemble a frieze. Furthermore, Peitersen's interpretation integrates the nature theme, which the school wants, and which is obvious from the school's natural surroundings. The coordination group's interpretation of art in learning is that it is free expression and more specifically, the children's free and personal expression, which is in contrast to the process they experienced in the art project.

Other subjects that point towards disagreement between an artistic and an educational perspective, are for example, the approach to the artistic supplies and resources, together with the artwork's specific or educational objective. For an artist, the "real" dimension is obvious – you work with a real painting, you get real tasks, which end with a real exhibition or public showing. Unfortunately, the pupils in the school are not used to creating something "for real" – their works often end up remaining within the school's domain (e.g. the essay is submitted to the teacher) and does not go beyond the school's domain. This project was different for all of the pupils at Andkær School because the artistic resources were "real" paint, not school materials and the objective was to create an authentic work of art that would be shown in a public space.

In regards to the educational objective, as stated earlier, Peitersen is unconcerned with learning as an output and if he does name anything along those lines, he refers specifically to abilities, techniques or signs of aesthetic understanding. This is contrary to the coordination group's interpretation of learning. Unfortunately, in this specific project, it was not possible to more specifically define the learning that the coordination group wanted to promote among their pupils.

The educators' recurring focus on quality is also evident in connection with the gap between the art culture and the school culture. The basic expectations that the coordination group had in regards to Peitersen's role, included quality assurance from a professional artist. During the project, the teachers discussed the following quality dilemma: Will we encourage the children to focus on details, be thorough with their artwork or will we just accept their work as this is "as good as it gets" and that their motor functions cannot allow more than that? Peitersen's answer to this question was that it may well be that small children cannot manage to do certain things "but they can see where something has to be done", i.e. they have a well-developed critical sense that they can employ and contribute with.

Hanne Pedersen interpreted her role in the Animation Workshop at Nørup School using a similar approach. As a supplement to the Peitersen's involvement at Andkær School, I can point out that Hanne Pedersen saw the creative process at the school as a joint project, where the focus was on the art's results. While the teachers perceive the help they can give to pupils as initiating activities and supplying ideas in the form of questions (we "get them going"): "Can you not use this here?", "Can you use a pencil case to keep pencils in?", Hanne's approach is much more nuanced. She "gets right behind them" and is not afraid to get involved in the creative process, whereas the teachers keep a pedagogical distance from the practical execution of the activities for the purpose of encouraging the children to do it themselves, to try things on their own. Unsurprisingly, Hanne, as a professional artist has an artistic point of view related to what the children produce and feels there is a higher meaning with a shared project. She feels that both the adults and children, teachers and pupils, experts and new beginners are in the same boat, which is driven by the art's arguments.

The artist's trust in the artistic process means she is not afraid to disturb the pupils' learning process or personal expression: "It'll be alright,", "We'll get there." Both the teachers and the artist agreed that art is a detour. If you link art to learning, then the path from A to B is longer, funnier, more creative, less manageable. Hanne's experiences with skewed artistic detours gives her confidence when managing complexity, while the teachers, as they ardently look for an educational output become confused.

As an observer, I thought at the beginning that Hanne's interpretation of her support role conflicted with the self-expression dimension that was also emphasised by the teachers. The self-expression dimension is defined here as the activities where individuals express themselves, their values and feelings. Nevertheless, Hanne explained in the interview that she believed children learn with an "eyes on" approach and not just with a "hands-on" approach. If the adult or expert or teacher acts as a role model and shows the children what they can develop, how to do it and how to use the subject's technical terms, the children learn from that, they become inspired and they develop their own version. By looking at a teacher (or I will add, by looking at each other, for example in *peer education*: See Damon, 1984, and Webb, 2010), the children acquire new knowledge which can be worked on and interpreted in specific applications.

In the Animation Project for example, the pupils saw the experts' methods of cutting figures, moving figures, animating and then they could do it themselves in their own way. The artist believes that the children's motivation is to "learn themselves", the teachers believe that motivation must always be stimulated. The teachers are therefore very focused on finding ways to motivate and engage the pupils.

Motivation theories (Amabile, 1996; Collins & Amabile, 1999) confirm the role that motivation has in learning and performance, though it is still much debated whether the classroom should make use of intrinsic (inner and detached from outputs) or extrinsic motivation (influences from the outside, basically divided in rewards or punishments).

Hanne's almost cultural deterministic[2] view of the children's learning is combined with an interpretation of the artistic media as expressive. As she puts it in her interview:

> I believe that most kids have a really, really strong urge to tell stories. And they are creative and animation as a media can provide them with a way of letting us follow their imagination, which is often not very logical. That is, they love to deny the laws of physics, get rid of everyday life and tell a more mythological reality, and animation as a media can do this and therefore they can do this, they can follow their crazy animated feature and their fantasy. And it, well I don't know, maybe it's something inherent in people, this desire to tell stories. So we cultivate this, so we sustain it through the school hours. And the animation as a media breathes fires into [it]. (Chemi, 2010a, p. 49)

2 Cultural determinism is defined as the belief that the culture we are raised in will strongly affect our emotions and our behaviour. This means that environmental effects have a greater influence on us than for example, biological or genetic elements.

Of course, as a teacher you believe the pupils wish to learn themselves, will express and create, as the artist says, it is a need we have inside us, the desire to tell a story, to express ourselves. Hanne's opinion is partly supported by theory, especially within the field of anthropology and evolutionary biology. For example, researcher Ellen Dissanayake contributed to an understanding of the necessity of art for humans on a biological basis (Dissanayake, 1995 and 2000; Chemi, 2009a).

On the other hand, the teachers have another approach where learning and the learning output are in focus, where the optimisation of time means that you have to achieve the outcome as quickly as possibly, where art is understood as a functional tool for generating learning and/or an engaging framework for learning; where the learning process develops rather than being an "add-on" experience and not as a going into depth, where the processes must be planned beforehand.

The teachers and artists appear to agree on the subject of art taking a longer path to learning. This perception is clearly evident in the focus group interview and even more pronounced in the interview with the teachers from Nørup School. In both cases, all of the adults agree that the artistic path to learning is a longer process. "Longer" in terms of the time it takes (it takes longer) and because educators need to activate several resources. As the teachers from Nørup School say, the learning processes "can be a bit of a detour". And as the artist says confidently: "We'll get there". However, adults and teachers need to ensure that the necessary conditions for supporting this process are in place and are prioritised and valued.

Why Artfulness?

Teachers and educators from the research project Artfulness, give a figurative answer to the above-mentioned question. They believe that art or art teaching is a kind of fancy cream topping, in contrast to real bread and butter education. This fancy cream topping that is art, makes lessons tasty, attractive and more pleasant.

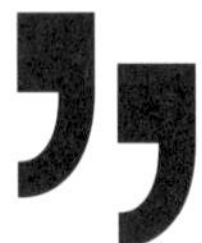

> If people knew,
> how hard I worked
> to get my mastery,
> it wouldn't seem
> so wonderful after all.
>
> Michelangelo

This metaphor has its drawbacks. Fancy cream toppings taste great but all those calories can be harmful and perhaps should be omitted from a healthy diet. If art in schools is a fancy cream topping, can we avoid it when the school doesn't require it to function efficiently? Like a dollop of cream in one's coffee or hot chocolate, is art a tasty but dispensable accompaniment? If the artistic subjects or activities are the equivalent of fancy cream topping, what are the academic subjects the equivalent of? In Scandinavia, the simple answer would be rye bread, sensible food that is full of nutritional goodness to get you through the day. In Denmark, regular tasks that include mundane daily routines and which are very boring are literally known as "rye bread work". Work that is physically hard and repetitive has led to "rye bread work" having negative associations, the way "donkey work" has negative associations in Britain.

The dichotomy between the meaning of the fancy cream topping and the rye bread metaphor runs the risk of missing certain important points when used to compare creative and academic subjects. By defining the artistic work processes as fancy cream topping, we run the risk of forgetting how much "rye bread work" is involved in the practice of art. For example, the length of time it takes for a pianist to learn scales and harmonies, the number of experiments needed for a painting to succeed, the number of performances and repetitions that an actor has to carry out before the premier, and so on.

There is also the risk of forgetting how much "fancy cream topping" there can be in an academic subject, how much enjoyment and pleasure can be derived from being engaged in, for example, English or mathematics. Or for example, how much curiosity and satisfaction can be generated by history, science or geography.

The reality is more complex than the cream topping/artistic subjects and rye bread/academic subjects metaphor would have it. This relationship is complicated further by a basic misunderstanding that is sometimes made by the public sector and even academics working within the artistic fields – the belief that visual texts do not need to be interpreted and learned on an equal basis with other (academic) texts.

This stereotypic view is based on two cultural beliefs. The first, is based on the separation of artistic and scientific subjects, which Herbert Spencer wrote about and advocated in an essay "What knowledge is of most worth?" that was published in 1860 (Spencer, 1966, pp. 121-159). This essay, which is a part of a comprehensive contribution about "education" from an evolutionary theory perspective (EDUCATION; *Intellectual, Moral, and Physical*), still influences Western society's perception of artistic forms, especially in relation to their role in teaching. Herbert Spencer was interested in using Darwin's theory of evolution within the field of education and at the same time he wanted to define industrial society's needs. The result was a new scientific hierarchy, where forms of art were considered purely as activities for entertainment compared to the serious occupations that were necessary for the survival and success of the human species, such as the scientific disciplines. According to this industrial ideology, artistic activities were considered a luxury, fancy cream topping, wholly dispersible and entirely related to emotions and personal taste. The academic separation of art and science (art versus science) educationally and at the level of scientific theory and philosophy has been heavily criticised (e.g. Reimer, 1992; Davis & Gardner, 1992; Robinson, 2009) because its underlying logic no longer corresponds with contemporary society's reality. The conviction that the school is a factory, whose objective is to create standardised workers, who know a lot about very little (specialists), was damaging enough in the 19th century but today, it is obsolete and unacceptable. According to Robinson (2009, p. 230) "public schools were not only created in the interest of industrialism - they were created in the image of industrialism. In many ways, they reflect the factory culture they were designed to support. This is especially true in high schools, where school systems base education on the principle of the assembly line and the efficient division of labor". Even though industrialisation has developed since the 19th century and our culture has moved towards globalisation, technology and an information society, we build the majority of our educational systems and institutions (from state school to university) based on an industrial and evolutionary model. This tendency damages both creativity and optimal learning that is based on an understanding of the subject and well-being.

The second conviction can be summed up as follows: Forms of art can be perceived through an immediate intuitive perception and do not require any further cognitive work. Visual works can be recognised in the blink of an eye, with little effort. At the same moment we see Leonardo's *Monna Lisa*, we have a feeling that we have understood the work because our perception functions almost automatically and in a fast, associative and effortless way (Kahneman, 2011). Nevertheless, we should emphasise that this immediate recognition does not necessarily lead to understanding, knowledge or higher consciousness if the individual is not actively engaged in deeper visual learning. The emotional or sensory perception and intuition does not necessarily lead to deep and retained reasoning or conceptual representations. In other words – art is and must be learned. The intuitive realisation is just *one* level within art's complex cognitive field, but for it to become learning, learners need to link this first level of comprehension with the rational comprehension, which is also embodied. Perhaps our impression is that we have understood *Monna Lisa* in a quick moment, but in reality we have only perceived it intuitively. If the sight of Leonardo's painting is guided towards a linguistic and more nuanced and controlled reasoning, then we are well on the way to experienced-based learning. The artistic experience – both pleasure and active creation – generates a complex field that is rich with optimal learning possibilities. These possibilities should be fully exploited in the schools.

The belief that individuals do not need to learn abilities and competencies in artistic subjects is often justified by the idea that it will "happen by itself." According to this approach, an aesthetic awareness will occur, either because the child is very gifted because of a genetically inherited talent for art or in the case of practical artistic activities with the children. People are indeed programmed to intuitively understand, for example pictures – but this is only partly correct. Talented young people are not only genetically predisposed,

Other creative resources as inspiration

www.wholechildeducation.org
www.sirkenrobinson.com

they are also stimulated and encouraged by their environment (family, school, friends, society) and practical activities in the school do not necessarily generate learning or development if the teachers do not ensure that this is the outcome. This means that the transfer of learning from an artistic experience to a cognitive understanding does just not "happen by itself" as a natural consequence of a *hands-on* activity.

To expect the natural transfer of learning is the equivalent of handing a child a book in German and saying: "Here. Read it!" and expect the child to be able to read the text and understand the meaning without any background knowledge. In the same way, we should not present a visual text to children and expect them to decode it without any background knowledge and training: "Here. 'Read' the picture!"

This attitude to learning is neither useful nor sound. But luckily, we can do something about it.

Teaching children how to understand visual imagery for example, is not just a good thing because the children think it is fun, it is a necessity because they live in a world that is dominated and saturated with visual texts. To integrate different art forms is not just fun because it allows self-expression, but also because the pupils become more aligned with the way the world expresses itself.

When schools have clarified the necessity of teaching art in a complex and rapidly changing world for the purpose of stimulating the whole person (holistic oriented teaching), they should also as practitioners in the artistic subjects find the correct arguments for supporting the case.

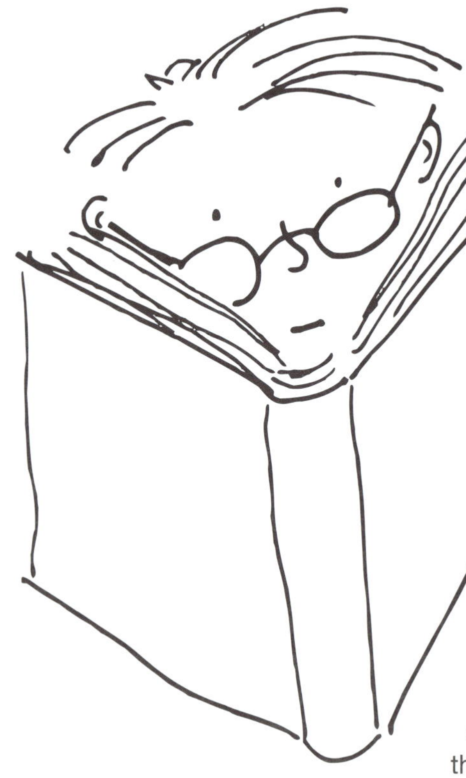

Figure 4 Reading competence

The viewpoint that is based on the claim that there is an automatic transfer of learning between the creative and the academic subjects, reveals a damaging attitude. Even though it may be very popular to emphasise, for example in music, because the children become better at mathematics by playing music, it is a false claim. First, research shows that if any kind of effect of that kind can be observed, it is limited and short-lived (Journal of Aesthetic Education, 2000). Second, it just does not happen like that. The way people learn and develop is a very complex and organic process. You just do not get A leading to B in a linear fashion. Music does not correspond with mathematical learning, unless in this connection it is guided and elaborated, but I will return to this point later. Only an obsolete industrial-school ideology can conceive of such an idea as above: That education is raw material driven into the factory at one end and the finished market-ready products are driven out the other end. Using the factory metaphor for schools will not get us very far in the future. The children do not come to school to be transformed into tomorrow's workers or users who all think alike and are "in boxes". They go to school to learn and develop and utilise their potential optimally. The statement music = mathematics opens up a non-systemic perception of reality and its complexity. Third, the above attitude holds on to an academic hierarchy, where academic subjects are at the top, given a value that makes them more important than the creative subjects, which lie somewhere at the bottom and are only worth bothering with as a way of supporting academic learning.

There are many good arguments that can support the use of art in teaching. However, schools should find the most suitable and productive, based on research and evidence. The perspective taken in this book, is that art can contribute to learning based on its structural combination of positive emotions and cognitive challenges, which supports the individual's biologically driven desire for well-being, learning and development.

The biological and psychological perspective

Among the many aesthetic theories that seek to explain why people practice art and why art is necessary for humanity (see Winner, 1982),

I will focus on an evolutionary and psychological perspective. Even though the two traditions use different logic and frameworks of understanding, they can be reconciled in their focus on the individual and the individual's ability to survive and to develop.

Anthropologist and evolutionary biologist Ellen Dissanayake, has examined the importance of art in human development, linking her research to what is special about being human from a biological and evolutionary perspective (2000, 1995).

As I have argued in other contributions (Chemi, 2014; Chemi, 2009a), Dissanayake links art to *intimacy* and explains the evolutionary background for people's need to create art and to enjoy art as a direct consequence of our ancestors' having raised themselves up on two legs and walked – *bipedality.* A side effect of this evolutionary move, was a number of biological, psychological and social elements relevant to survival.

The upright position which was more effective for several activities also had a number of drawbacks. The female's hips became smaller and children's brains grew, to be able to deal with nature's complexities and challenges. The evolutionary process saw the female develop more flexible hips and the infant gained a fontanel ("any of the spaces closed by membranous structures between the uncompleted angles of the parietal bones and the neighbouring bones of a foetal or young skull"; Webster, 1989), which meant that the large cranium in infants was flexible enough for the birthing process.

The perfect evolutionary logic had made human infants more vulnerable and helpless for a longer period of time compared to other mammals: Emotional attachment (emotionality) and the mother-child reciprocity became a question of survival. If the mother could not become emotionally attached to her baby then her care for the child would not be persistent enough to ensure its survival. Furthermore, reciprocity, *bonding* and *emotionality* are the basis for another basic survival strategy – the establishment of social relationships with other human beings.

This has meant that humans are special not just because we live in societies, but because we are able to specialise (*handiness*), we are able to learn from each other and we are deeply dependent on these activities. Many other animals live in clans or groups and some of them use tools – even though it is clear that humans' toolmaking skills are far more advanced – and nearly all animals can learn as they grow but only humans' survival are so dependent on these abilities.

And this is why humans had to find specific strategies: According to this theory, art was one of those strategies. Art was able to affect all of the elements and phases in peoples' lives, which Dissanayake defines as *making special*.

Humans are the only species able to make cognitive abstractions and to be interested in them, for example, symbols, aesthetic design, imagination and innovation. If we transfer Dissanayake's categorisation of *making special* into the aesthetic field, then almost all examples of human artistic production can be used as examples.

Rituals or ritual behaviours, which are the source for art (Turner, 1967), are built on the need to make any given element special. The same happens in specific artistic experiences. If for example, we look at dance as an art form, we are able to recognise the symbolic movements that correspond to our everyday movements. But hopping, jumping, rhythmic patterns, etc. make the everyday movements special by giving them more meaning and a different quality: movements in dance are bigger or smaller than in everyday life, or just more grotesque or harmonic, less balanced or less functional. Turner speaks for a theoretical approach that advocates emotional positivity in art, using the term *liminality*. According to Turner, people have also used rituals for the purposes of signalling a transition from one condition to another, which the individual and tribe find meaningful. This transformation is experienced as being crucial for the individual's cultural and social development. If Aristotle's' *catharsis* is reminiscent of the modern therapeutic approach to art, Turner's view of art is closer to a term like the general process of socio-cultural development. The journey through art's liminality, informs the individual through a necessary (and often positive and desirable) self-development.

Art psychology has a slightly different perspective, which explains the unique in art in many different ways. I will mainly focus on two positions: Art as pleasure and art as knowledge. The first is also called the "arousal" theory because it focuses on pleasure that people feel in response to art's formal elements ("pleasure given by art's formal properties"; Winner, 1982, p. 64). The second perspective, also called the cognitive, focuses on art's usefulness: "Art serves the human need for knowledge [and] functions ultimately to reveal and clarify reality" (Winner, 1982, p. 65). The two psychological paths can, as readers will discover in the next chapters, be brought together in flow theory (Csikszentmihalyi, 1990; 2000). To sum up, let us return to the question "Why Artfulness?" The answer is because artistic creative processes and craftsmanship have always been a means to satisfying the most intangible and subconscious biological and psychological human needs.

In the next chapters, I will take a closer look at the special combination of positive emotions and cognitive challenges.

Positive emotions

Feelings and emotions are described differently in the fields of psychology and philosophy (Goldie, 2002). Sometimes the two terms are synonymous, and sometimes their domains are separated. The aim of this book is not to examine this complex hermeneutic challenge but to offer a working definition that can be used as a framework of understanding. In this book, emotions and feelings are understood as two sides of the same coin, not as separate domains (sensory versus conceptualisation), but closer to a holistic phenomenon. Damasio (1994) has for example, contributed to this understanding by looking at the emotions' essence as material, physical and sensory. Damasio conceptually separates emotions and feelings but considers them as two sides of the same neurological process. The essence of emotions are changes in bodily state, which arise from a person's thoughts or reactions to their thoughts. On the other hand, the essence of feelings are the perception that we connect with physical changes before there is an emotional response. If emotions are "the collection of changes in body state connected to particular mental images" (Damasio, 1994, p. 145), so feelings are "the process of continuous monitoring, that experience of what your body is doing while thoughts about specific contents roll by" (ibid.). Damasio' taxonomy separates three different emotional inputs, feelings that arise from universal emotions (e.g. joy, anger, fear), experience-based emotions (e.g. ecstasy, euphoria), feelings that can be neutral, in the case of background feelings, "the feeling of life itself, the sense of being" (Damasio, 1994, p. 150). Furthermore, emotions can be primarily or secondary. Primary emotions are defined above, whereas secondary emotions are those emotional reactions to others' feelings and are often the cause of those beliefs that we have about experiencing specific feelings. The secondary emotions are thus determined by culture, for example a person can feel ashamed as a result of angst or sadness or fear, depending on the personal and cultural beliefs he or she adds. In this respect, some emotions may be interpreted as positive or negative, depending on the culture you are in.

I will furthermore refer to Fredrickson & Branigan's definition of emotions because of its insights into learning and self-development. The two researchers define emotions as short-term experiences that produce changes in the individual's thoughts, actions and physiological reactions: "Emotions are short-lived experiences that produce coordinated changes in people's thoughts, actions, and physiological responses" (Fredrickson & Branigan, 2005, pp. 313-332). The two researchers have studied the cognitive effects of emotions, when they are positive or perceived as such and they have found clear correlations between the experience of positive emotions and learning.

Fredrickson & Branigan define positive emotions as feelings that are able to develop the individual's cognitive field: "broaden the scopes of attention, cognition, and action, widening the array of percepts, thoughts, and actions presently in mind" (2005, p. 315).

Fredrickson's research agrees well with the neuroscience that finds links between emotions and learning. According to these studies (Immordino-Yang & Fisher, 2009; Immordino-Yang & Damasio, 2007), there are good grounds to see the emotions as a fundamental element of learning. An obsolete view of emotions saw them as being "like a toddler in a china shop, interfering with the orderly rows of stemware on the shelves" (Immordino-Yang & Damasio, 2007, p. 4), but experimental studies show "the critical role of emotion in bringing previously acquired knowledge to inform real-world decision making in social contexts [and] that emotional processes are required for the skills and knowledge acquired in school to transfer to novel situations and to real life" (Immordino-Yang & Damasio, 2007, p. 5). Brain damage in individuals that were not able to activate the emotional processes, also seemed to have affected their ability to learn optimally: Even though they did not display any loss of logic or ethical knowledge, they were not able to solve problems, make decisions and transfer learning in others contexts or *real-life* contexts.

Positive emotions appear to be active means of developing individual strengths, and for building resilience and robustness (Luthar, 2006). When the individuals feel robust, they are capable of learning in an optimal way, which is effective and light, i.e. learning is remembered, utilised and desired. In Fredrickson & Branigan (2005), this learning can be stimulated via positive emotions, because they generate thoughts that are:

- Unusual
- Flexible and inclusive
- Creative
- Integrative
- Open to information
- Effective

All of the above qualities are necessary in learning situations: If an individual cannot be open to information, it will be impossible to learn, if the pupils are not open to unusual, creative and flexible thoughts, they will not learn anything new and creative, without inclusive, integrating and effective learning, it is not possible to achieve optimal learning. Emotions and intellectual challenges are so closely related that the two together can contribute to learning processes. But how does art and this positive synergy hang together?

When observing pupils who are involved in arts programmes or activities, their enjoyment and engagement are clearly visible. But to link artistic experiences with emotional happiness is really a stereotypical perception. What lies behind this romantic stereotype that connects art with positive emotions and emotions in general? What lies behind the emotion-laden discourse, when art is experienced in the schools?

Above all, I should explain that not all of the emotions individuals experience in the encounter with art are positive, but all emotions can have a positive effect within the artistic experiences and therefore are experienced or remembered as positive. Even the negative emotions have their positive role to play in the experience of art, a role that is interpreted differently in specific knowledge theories. Negative emotions are a necessary step in every process where the individual develops spiritually or intellectually and gains self-knowledge and learns about the world or a given subject: "[…] when we do not allow ourselves to experience painful emotions, we limit our capacity of happiness" (Ben-Shahar, 2009, p. xvii). To limit our ability to experience negative or positive emotions is the equivalent of limiting our ability to learn and develop, which are necessary conditions for experiencing inquisitiveness, interest, engagement and to be able to further absorb and process information. This gradation between positive emotions and the positive effects of negative emotions in a learning perspective and the empirical knowledge that it is based on has not been my main focus in this book. Nevertheless, this theme should be examined further because it is very relevant for a nuanced understanding of emotions in learning and education.

The art technique known as *chiaroscuro* may be used as a specific metaphor to describe the relationship between positive and negative emotions. This technique was discovered in the Renaissance period, where artists used bold contrasts between light and dark (*chiaroscuro* is an Italian word that literally means light-dark) in their drawings or paintings. A painter who uses this technique is not just interested in light but also to a high degree, he or she is interested in darkness, which provides a strong contrast and intensifies the bright areas in a picture. In a *chiaroscuro* painting, the dark and bright areas cannot exist without each other and only their dialogue is able to create meaning and feelings. *Chiaroscuro* is for painting what Fredrickson's *positivity ratio* is for positive psychology, an explanation of how positive/light and negative/dark interrelate. Fredrickson further qualified this relationship as a 3:1 ratio, where three positive experiences were required for a person to forget one negative experience (2009). Developed on the basis of mathematical equations and evidence that has since been criticised and reviewed (Brown, Sokal, & Friedman, 2013; Fredrickson, 2013), this ratio makes the role of negative emotions visible. It emphasises the fact that negative emotions are as important to development as positive emotions are. Just as *chiaroscuro* emphasises the play between light and darkness, which can be a targeted meaning and meaningful artistic experience, the dialectics between positive and negative emotions are fundamental for the very essence of being human.

The Artfulness study findings have clearly confirmed that art experiences in school settings are able to create a positive emotional attitude among the participating individuals. Both teachers and pupils report a number of positive feelings and emotions. But what type of emotions have specifically been reported?

The focus on the pupils' perspective has emphasised that the experienced emotions within the artistic projects have been assessed as being strong, and among the emotions that were experienced, several are recurring:

- Joy
- Engagement
- Flow

Joy

Among the different types of joy the interviewed pupils report, there is an intensity that grows from "comfort" to "excitement". The pupils assess the educational initiative that they have participated in as being positive and their emotional state is similarly positive. These different types of joyful states can be defined as:

- **Cognitive joy**: The pupils experience cognitive enjoyment when they report or clearly show a generic desire to move deeper into the intellectual and emotional activity. In this case, the children become joyful when they experience that the artistic activity makes them think and/or feel. For example, the educators from Andkær School reported that the artist they had worked with had caused the children "to think".
  - Instrumental joy of learning: A sub-category of cognitive joy can be the satisfaction that the pupils experience when the artistic activity helps them to learn something that is specifically related to school. For example, when the pupils from Nørup School link their newly discovered learning about grammar or mathematics with an emotionally positive state.

- **Joy of recognition**: For example, when the pupils from Andkær School are taken through the town in search of works of art and experience a positively felt state when recognising things they had seen before or already knew about. Or when pupils from Engum School draw a layout based on their general knowledge about how to build a house or furnish a room. Another aspect of the joy of recognition is the possibility of making personal connections between a work of art and personal life experiences. When the work of art "talks to me", when I can see or recognise myself and my life story, it creates a unique emotional and existential bond between the individual and the work of art.

- **Joy of comprehension**: For example, when the pupils from Nørup School grasp a grammatical rule or mathematical formula more easily and more effectively by solving a task in Danish or mathematics using animation as a tool.

- **Joy of expression**: Art forms are often linked to freedom of expression and feelings. A quick literary review of art-related trends of the last 100 years shows that this linking of art and feelings or freedom of expression starts in the Romantic Period (see Winner, 1982; Harrison, Wood & Gaiger, 1998; Harrison & Wood, 1992; Murray, 2003). Looking at the empirical data from this study, I have observed a special state of satisfaction when the pupils were able to freely express themselves. This is contrasted with the frustration that was reported when the artistic activities did not include the possibility of the pupils being able to express themselves (see Chemi 2010b).

- **Hedonistic joy**: Interviews, researcher observations and the teachers' observations point to a pure hedonistic enjoyment. The pupils look enthralled at the artworks' sensory quality and are absorbed in the artistic processes and the material. Several times, the pupils from Andkær School reported their excitement over the colours and the impressive size of the artwork. Similarly, the pupils from Engum School, Nørup School and U School[3] seemed to enjoy the artistic and sensory quality of the artworks and artistic processes.

- **Interpersonal joy**: The main objective of all of the artistic activities observed in the Artfulness study was to create a work of art that could be enjoyed by others – a musical, animation, a mural, a prototype of a house, a picture frame, etc. The work process included both the individual's and the group's contributions. The majority of the pupils were positive about this collective work process, reporting that they were very happy with the collaborative interaction between ages and genders. Furthermore, the "public" dimension of their artworks (all works were to be exhibited, staged or presented within the school environment) also made them happy and proud.

This empirical-based taxonomy overlooks two important types of happiness, which the literature in art psychology, art education and art therapy otherwise focuses a great deal on (Winner, 1982; Knill, Levine & Levine, 2005): Therapeutic joy and joy resulting from the personal

3 In addition to the schools I have named, other schools in Vejle Municipality contributed to the Artfulness project. These schools, whose roles were marginal to the study, are mentioned anonymously.

development process. These two types of joy, which are meaningful from a theoretical perspective are only mentioned here and not thoroughly discussed because these two functions were not reported by the interviewees or observed during the field observations in the Artfulness project.

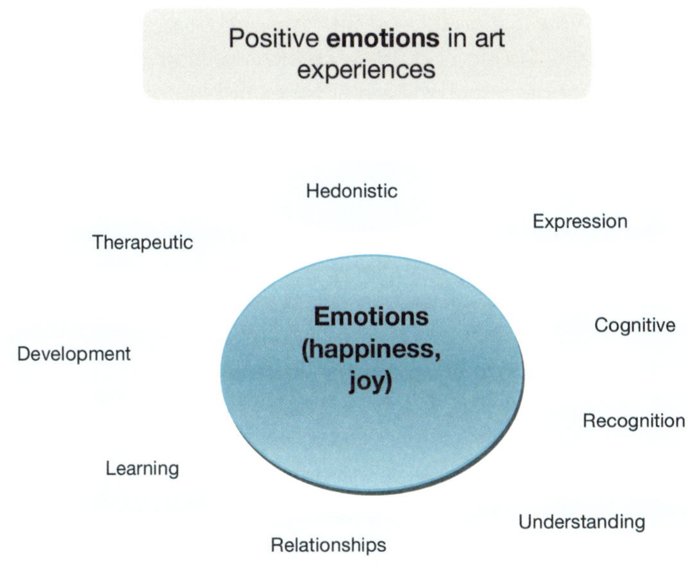

Figure 5 Positive emotions in arts participation

Engagement

According to the pupils at Andkær School, the project has been fun and difficult: "We had fun but the work was still hard", "There wasn't anything [about the project] that was especially easy but some of it was more difficult than other bits". Pupils felt that they had "worked hard" (Chemi, 2011).

Despite the effort, they felt they had been suitably challenged and were given the support they needed. At the same time, they experienced clear and well-defined frameworks. As they say, "We would have taken our morning break if we weren't told what we had to do" (ibid.). In other words, if their task had not been explained clearly to them, they would have taken their breaks all of the time. This shows there was a high level of flow, which both my observations and the pupils' statements confirm. The good balance between having fun and feeling comfortable, or experiencing positive emotions and having difficulty, i.e. positive challenges, is characteristic of a flow experience. In Csikszentmihalyi's definition, flow is a positive state, *"beyond boredom and anxiety"* (Csikszentmihalyi, 2000), and these children neither experienced the negative side of boredom because of for example, too few challenges and too little to do, neither did they become fearful because of overwhelming challenges.

Similarly, neither did the pupils on Engum School's KDH (art, design, crafts) course or the pupils at Nørup School's Animation Workshop have time to take a break. However, so much engagement in a school culture that is not flexible can lead to frustrations, which some of the above mentioned pupils experienced. Even though Engum School's KDH (art, design, crafts) structure was more flexible than general classes, the breaks were fixed in the timetable and the pupils who were experiencing good work flow at the break times were asked to take their breaks anyway.

The pupils at Nørup School were so involved in their work that they simply did not have time to take a break. As one child explained: "We don't have time to go out and play football. We have lots of ideas. If we don't do it now they'll disappear!" (Chemi, 2011, p. 56). Luckily, the structure of the workshop was flexible enough that it worked out okay, but the teachers' dilemma in trying to transform this structure into general learning is very understandable.

Andkær School has really pushed the envelope in their experimentation with a working model that broke with the school set-up by coordinating the artistic collective activities in a natural synergy with the play activities. The pupils could at any time move from one activity to another (play and art), owning their own contributions to the artwork as a joint project.

As a teacher, what do you specifically do when you meet such a scale of engagement in the pupils' contribution to a project, where they do not have time or want to take their break? How do you balance this with the fixed school timetable? How do you integrate a flexible project structure within the fixed school timetable? These dilemmas arise in all of the project schools and remain open topics of reflection within the creative teaching forms.

Flow

On the basis of the theoretical considerations about flow, described in the flow literature (among others, Csikszentmihalyi, 2000), this book includes flow states under the term *positive emotions*. Both my understanding of flow studies and the teachers perception of flow are about a positive and deep state of individual concentration. To the teachers and educators, this state appears to be very desirable. Informal interviews with Artfulness informants indicate that they value it when their pupils show or report a positive flow experience. Some schools even regarded generating flow experiences as the main objective of their development project (e.g. School B).

Flow

A positive state of concentration and falling away of self-awareness, which is a result of the experience of reaching a balance between the challenges the individual faces and the individual's ability to meet those challenges (see the flow model in Figure 16).

Even though the Artfulness-study's objective was not specifically to measure or describe flow experiences, this term turned up frequently in connection with the positive evaluation of the arts activities.

The pupils themselves reported several times a positive balance between challenges (the difficulty of the artistic challenge) and their ability to deal with challenges (the joy, excitement and engagement they have experienced). In addition, the pupils reported that they were in no doubt about what they had to do: Sign of clear and meaningful frameworks, which are a prerequisite for flow experiences.

In one case, I have tried to test the pupils' flow level with an ad-hoc questionnaire (described in Chemi, 2009b, 2012, 2013). This flow experiment took place at Engum School, because I had observed that not only was it quiet, which the teachers had reported in the research interview and in an interview with a journalist (Eriksen, 2009), there was even a special "buzzing" sound. By integrating performance analysis with flow studies, I noticed a special buzzing sound, almost like the sound from a beehive. The sound is high enough that observers can hear it but not high enough to be noise, a constant, almost unbroken tone over a longer period of time, uninterrupted rhythm, regardless of which activity was being carried out (paper and pencil tasks, group work, reading, creating material, tasks on digital media).

Using the same observation methods, I also noticed that the pupils' movement in the room followed a regular and specific pattern when they took over the room, which I define as "centripetal". The term is used in physics and defines a movement towards a centre in opposition to a centrifugal force whose line of direction is away from the centre.

In the case of independent tasks, both individual and group tasks, the pupils link to a "centre" of activity, this can be a place where the child reads, writes, draws, etc. or where the group discusses, works with a PC, etc. – a centre is there where the activity unfolds. Especially in the case of group work it is important that all of the pupils feel that they are "attracted" to what is going on in the centre of the activity. If this does not happen, the pupils move away from their workstation and find other interesting things outside the task: This is often the case for children, who begin to disturb the other children or groups or who leave the class, which means the teachers must go out and bring them back.

It is worth noting that this centripetal/centrifugal dynamic can have a physical and a psychological nature. In the case of the latter, the children lose concentration, and this leads to other results, e.g. the "ordinary, private chat [...] with football, with that [they] shall play football", as the teachers put it (Chemi, 2009b). On the other hand, it was observed that there was a general absence of this "private chat" in the KDH project at Engum School, which benefited a school-related dialogue "where they respected and listened to what was being said in the group, and reached agreement and shall find a solution" (ibid.).

On 19 February 2009, both I and the teachers at Engum School saw a high level of engagement and contemplation in the activity and I remarked that there was a clear "buzzing sound" and centripetal movement in the room.

The teachers and I therefore decided to test our impression and ask the children about their experience. The purpose of asking the children at the end of the day was to see whether our observation was confirmed or disproved. This was the reason why a detailed analysis of the responses was not carried out, because the objective was to emphasise the average in relation to boys and girls (which was the only noted variable) and in relation to the activity at hand.

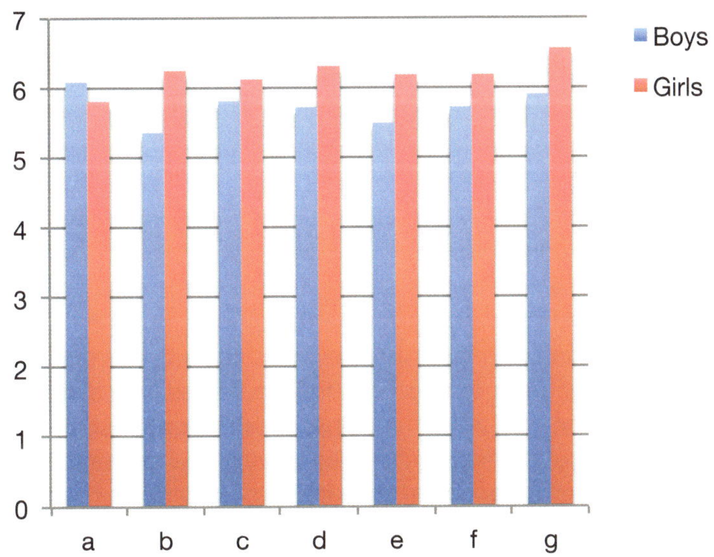

Figure 6 Flow experience: Average 19 February 2009

The data was interpreted in accordance with Andersen (2008): "A score of 5 or over with a minimum of five statements is assessed as indicating that the pupil's school activities for the respective day had flow, i.e. the potential for learning and satisfaction were very ripe, while an average between 3.0 and 4.9 indicated there was a good basis for learning and satisfaction with some flow, and an average score of below 3.0 indicated the potential was less favourable" (my translation from Danish). The results show that all of the children on average have experienced a good flow level of about 6.0 and several individual responses were well over the average among girls and boys (however, less so among the boys). [4]

Another limited flow study was carried out at Engum School on 26 February 2009 for the purposes of comparison with the same subproject about architecture. At that point, the children had been involved in the architecture task for a longer consecutive period of time, thus they had started to lose a little interest in the activity, which was clear from my observation of the first part of the morning activity and in the flow measurements.

The level of engagement and level of concentration was still high, but the trend was falling (5.9 for the girls, 5.6 for the boys). Nevertheless, the expert's visit (a professional architect who was to assess the pupils' work and provide guidance) had a positive effect on some of the individual responses, bringing flow back up again (6.0 for the girls and 5.8 for the boys), a trend that was confirmed by the ethnographic observations.

Surprisingly, some of the pupils gave a low assessment of the second part of the morning that was spent with the expert. The reason for this can be found in the children's interviews. Those who did not get personal feedback from the architect because of time constraints, still remember the day as a frustrating experience and still remark that there was some dissatisfaction and a sense of unfairness.

4 All of the responses are shown in the appendixes in Chemi, 2009b and in Chemi 2012, 2013.

What the teachers and I have learned from this mini flow study, is that the pupils in general were very self-sufficient and motivated, probably because of the good balance between fixed frameworks and flexibility (flow preconditions), which appears to have contributed to the positive development. Furthermore, the artistic activities appear to have motivated and engaged the pupils, thus they could themselves experience and report a positive state of concentration and falling away of self-awareness.

Anything goes?

Lastly, in regards to the positive emotions that the pupils experienced during the observed development projects within the Artfulness project, a frequent occurring reaction to these experiences should be noted. Their positive assessment of the process that they had experienced was often based on the generic "anything goes" approach. That is, when they were asked what was positive about the process, they answered "being able to do something that was different", "being outside", learning "in a different way" (Chemi, 2011). At first glance these statements may cause us to suspect there had been a "Hawthorne-like effect".

Even though the Artfulness study was not experimental (i.e. no controlled experiments were carried out at the schools), I have asked myself if a Hawthorne-like effect was in play and had affected the data analysis. For example, on several occasions the pupils at Andkær School (but also at B

HAWTHORNE EFFECT

The *Hawthorne effect* is defined as a tendency in empirical studies for when a research observation affects the research field it is observing. Between 1927 and 1932, a group of researchers from Harvard University carried out a number of studies at the Hawthorne Works based outside Chicago. These studies were carried out to see if the productivity of the employees improved if some specific conditions were changed. Controlling the higher or lower level of light, the results showed a surprising trend: Both the intervention group and the control group's showed a positive effect. Specifically, the observed subjects changed their behaviour because they believed that they were being observed because the researchers and the organisation were interested in them and not in the intervention (Wickström & Bendix, 2000). Regardless of the changes that were introduced, productivity went up, in a sort of socially shared placebo effect.

School, which participated to a lesser degree in the study and anonymously) stated the project's positive outcome in these terms: "great to try something new", "it's been fun trying something new [...] and to get some change" (Chemi, 2011). According to the pupils statements, the art project appears to have had an impact on the children because it was new and different.

On the other hand, the pupils understood that the project had a specific value in addition to its novelty value. When I asked a pupil if the experience had been as much fun as playing football, the pupil answered that it would not have been the same: "First, I'm not really into playing football. [...] We also work together in a way that's better [...]. It's not just about being outside, it's also about they way we work" (ibid.). Unfortunately, this pupil did not have the opportunity to reflect over his experience and his feeling for a good work process and therefore cannot fully articulate the experience.

If we put these responses into perspective with that which the different projects have in common, we can assume that the pupils are happy because of the ways for learning and working that breaks away from classrooms, books and fixed and rigid frameworks. Therefore these statements should not be understood as indifference ("anything goes") but as a long awaited change to the school timetable and to the educational design. The pupils appear to have finally been released, able to breathe and to enjoy the change, which challenges them both academically, emotionally and socially as a whole. It appears that they were very receptive and could easily take on these creative challenges and they reacted with inquisitiveness and enthusiasm. If their fervour could be directed to all of the new forms or learning, regardless of whether it was about artistic projects or not, it does not necessarily mean that the pupils are indifferent to what they occupy their time with but perhaps that they are tired of the general approach to learning. I believe that these assessments are important warning signs for the schools of tomorrow who want to develop their pupils in a creative and engaged way. And it should be taken seriously.

Teachers' own positive emotions

The pupils' enthusiasm for the art-based forms of teaching reflect the teachers' enthusiasm. The teachers and kindergarten teachers that have been involved in the artistic development projects within the Artfulness project, take on new roles during the teaching, they are guides, facilitators and fellow learners. The teachers at Engum School report a greater amount of energy in the work and a rediscovered enthusiasm for their subjects. Furthermore, they report a greater desire to learn, which is clearly expressed in their efforts for personal and academic development.

Similarly, the other teachers are positive about their learning and participating role in the projects. I assume that the experienced positive result for the process and the project's completion has a large influence on the adults' positive attitude. The teachers and educators finished their projects with a satisfying feeling of complete success and that this can only be expected to have a positive effect on their emotional response to the project.

They express and show a great deal of satisfaction and joy. When the question "Which positive emotions or feelings inspires art for you as an individual or teacher and for your pupils?" was asked in the focus group interview, the following answers were given:

- Art is valuable
- Art is meaningful
- Pride
- Solidarity
- You experience that "I am seen" – myself seen as the whole person.
- You can learn that you can learn without the teacher.

The teachers emphasise here the positive emotions that the individuals feel when they are engaged in valuable and meaningful initiatives, which the artworks represent. They name the feelings of pride for the works that they create or the processes that they helped to create and a feeling of positive solidarity. Finally, the teachers name two cognitive approaches: A positive experience that is about being treated as an individual as a whole person and an educational co-ownership and independence.

It is very indicative that the teachers' answers also show them thinking a great deal about their pupils or the learning and the positive experiences that they were able to stimulate as teachers with help from art. The teachers and educators experience positive emotions by creating a positive learning environment for their pupils. Much of their experienced joy thus depends on their ability to get through to the pupils and to get happy pupils who learn well.

When the teachers had to report about their pupils' emotional responses to the artistic development projects that they participated in, they sound more nuanced than their pupils. The diverse forms of positive emotions are articulated in the interviews with the teachers:

- Desire to be involved
- Flow
- Engagement
- Perseverance
- Enthusiasm
- Co-ownership
- Successes based on own experiences by experimenting with hands-on experiences.
- Mutual respect and receptiveness and at the same time a democratic approach to finding common solutions and to reaching agreement and compromise.
- Positive thinking "instead of blocking some things because at first you don't think it can be done" (Chemi, 2011).
- Fun and engagement: They think it is exciting to be involved.

According to the formal interviews with Andkær School's kindergarten teachers and informal interviews with the teachers, the development project has been "very valuable" because the pupils were so engaged. The teachers observed that the children were eager and wanted to get going without waiting on the teachers' instructions, they were brave and jumped right in. The teachers were in fact surprised by how the pupils "stood around the panels [to be painted] and talked together" (ibid.), and they could see that the pupils developed. At Engum School as well, the teachers could see the pupils' excitement and Nørup School's teachers point out a specific target group that appears to have benefited in particular with the new teaching platform – the "weak" pupils who do not normally thrive during learning.

The pupils became happy because they could both learn and have fun, because they could escape from the everyday boredom, because they experienced "something else" at school. The teachers became happy because the pupils were happy, they considered that in itself a success criterion and because they knew and could experience that the pupils were getting better at learning. This supports the theories and studies that interpret art as a cognitive phenomenon: The enjoyment we feel when we experience art comes from an awareness that we have actually learned something new, have grasped a rule, have become cleverer (see Winner, 1982).

This is a sign of a positive, caring culture and my impression is that this is something that is cultivated in Denmark. At all of the schools that I visited during the Artfulness project, I could see educators who cared about and were attentive to the pupils' needs and psychological and emotional well-being. The teachers' intuition regarding the need for a renewal of the school system, means that the Artfulness project schools are good examples of the fight against boredom. As many studies about Danish schools (see Knoop, 2009a) and international contribution to good learning (Ritchhart, 2002; Robinson, 2001) show, the educational system's worst enemy is boredom. The pupils often report, across ages and cultures, that they are bored in school. Therefore, the schools within the Artfulness project are good examples of when teachers dare to experiment with alternative teaching models and learning know-how.

Nevertheless, we should be aware that positive emotions is not the only objective with experimental arts projects or with the inclusion of art in teaching. This approach can be problematic because it shows a low level of ambition, which does not match the major learning potential inherent in the world of art.

Cognitive Intensity

The pupils in the observed Artfulness projects have reported that the outcome was more than just enjoyment and happiness. From a motivation theory perspective, we know that learning and joy are interrelated, so that a positive emotional experience can increase and strengthen a learning outcome. Learning is most effective when the learning process is pleasurable in itself and both learning and positive emotions are self-reinforcing, i.e. the more positive the learning an individual experiences the more inclined the individual is to learn. The more positive emotions we feel, the more we want to learn.

Therefore, the cognitive and the emotional outcome cannot be separated. In the artistic experiences, these two aspects are bound together even more tightly, because each respectively is an outcome of the artistic experiences but also linked with each other as self-reinforc-

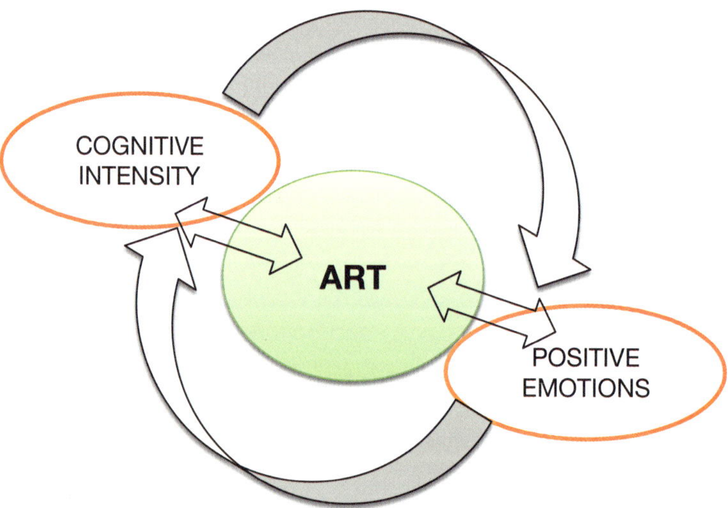

Figure 7 Synergy cognition and emotion in arts experiences

ing units. For example, a child may experience hedonistic happiness when working with colours, painting and large meaningful artworks, where the child who can express himself and at the same time learn something about art, for example English, history and geometry. This child will learn and be joyful at the same time. When the artistic activities end, the child will presumably sit with an inner desire to experience more of these positive emotions.

Similarly, the pupils in the Artfulness project experienced a large learning outcome, strengthened by the positive emotional framework.

Which types of cognitive challenges have these projects stimulated in the pupils? Have they been intellectually challenging? What learning did the pupils report?

In the current section, I define cognitive intensity as a state where the individual feels intellectually challenged at an appropriate and manageable level. The intensity results in the experienced challenges being slightly more difficult or completely unmanageable. In flow terms, the individual experiences the intensity when he or she moves further out from his comfort zone, in towards the engaging challenges. The individual experiences it as a small push in the back, to step over his or her intellectual limits. The flow model visualises the cognitive intensity as a wave that moves in and out of the flow channel and which is orientated towards a high degree of difficulty (see Figure 16). The intensity also stems from a qualitative complexity of the phenomenon: The individual can feel himself challenged on many different intellectual or academic levels.

In the Artfulness project, we can see a trend where the children have been intellectually engaged and challenged: They are able and willing to sit for longer periods of time and concentrate on the given tasks even though it may be difficult. This in itself shows us that the intellectual work has been very rewarding and that they have actually learned something. It shows that they have "worked hard". In their interviews, the pupils named the following learning areas:

- Academic subjects
- Technical tools from the different forms of art
- Mindset

Numeracy and literacy subjects

When the pupils are engaged in a process that combines academic and creative subjects, the artistic frameworks are able to facilitate a deeper and better academic learning. For example, the teachers at Nørup School developed a process where the main task, which was to make a short animation film, included different smaller academic tasks. The instructions were clear and specific from the beginning, where both the teachers and the participating animation artists articulated the limited academic tasks as "Danish" and "mathematics". It resulted in the pupils themselves noting that they had learned something about adjectives, nouns, verbs and mathematics.

This is coherent with the studies regarding the transfer of academic knowledge or learning based on artistic practices, which shows that a transfer of learning cannot be documented unless the teachers themselves ensure that they make it explicit (Journal of Aesthetic Education, 2000). For example, that the teachers should explicitly introduce the learning experience based on art as teaching in Danish or mathematics, if they integrated these subjects. If the set framework is unclear to the pupils, educators risk creating doubt and confusion. For example, as the pupils at School B asked: "What has today got to do with mathematics?" (unpublished interview, Vejle Municipality, 2010), despite the teachers' intention that mathematics would be taught through play. Children (and adults to some degree too) are often not able to link an aesthetic experience to academic learning without clear references that this is the intention.

Furthermore, the interpretation of research data regarding a "natural" transfer of learning from the artistic experiences to the academic subjects is very problematic. The research does not show a clear and sustained causality between artistic practice and high achievement in school. In other words, we cannot claim that the pupils become better a mathematics by playing music. The research evidence shows that if you want the pupils to get better at mathematics, you have to train them in mathematics. Nevertheless, there is such rich learning potential within artistic experiences that by integrating the academic subjects with the artistic frameworks educators can create an engaging, attractive and challenging learning environment. But in this case, educators must make this integration explicit, just as the teachers at Nørup School did with the Animation Workshop.

Similarly, the teachers from Engum School and Nørup School report that the pupils appear to have absorbed the deeper teaching that goes "under the skin", learning "which they did not [have] previously. They get a supplement to some of the techniques they have previously [learned]. They learn [...] to combine some of the possibilities that exist in the subjects that we offer" (Chemi, 2011). The pupils remember better and understand to a greater degree the academic subjects involved while at the same time, they experience the learning process as light, fun and meaningful.

This engages the pupils so much that they take responsibility for their own learning and participate actively in the learning process. Because they are allowed to be part of the creative process from the beginning, they develop a sense of co-ownership during both the creative and learning process.

Technical tools from the various art forms

In respect of the specific knowledge about the type of art that has been in focus in the individual development projects, the pupil's interviews reveal that they have learned a great deal: The pupils at Engum School explain that they have used their knowledge from KDH (art, design, crafts) in their everyday life and their games at home, the pupils from U School practice music in their free time, the pupils from Nørup School rattle off a detailed list of the technical-artistic tools they have learned to use.

The former pupils show an assimilation of an optimal learning, i.e. a learning that becomes competency and which can be used in new contexts (Bruner, 1973). For these children, this learning is meaningful because they can see specific applications which are obviously desirable: They report a clear desire to learn more within KDH (art, design, crafts) and a special satisfaction with the new teaching method and inquisitiveness about its content.

"I learned tons. For example, to make pauses and I've learned that you mustn't stick your head or hand above the table, floor or paper and I've learned to save the films", "I've learned how to take pictures and how you get the figures to move" and "also to use the computer and camera", [I've learned] to hold pauses", "to add sound to the film", "to start up and delete" (Chemi, 2011). All of these statements from the pupils' interviews at Nørup School document a clear consciousness about a professional competency, which is very specific, very practical, enjoyable and immediately useful.

In a time when schools are hit by cutbacks and lay-offs, or where the public sector expectations focus on the streamlining of teaching and the measuring of results, this type of teaching is perhaps not valued. When the pupils are to be measured in terms of PISA results, what value has the learning that the pupils get from art? Why should a teacher choose to "waste" time with subjects that the pupils are not tested in? Learning experts Howard Gardner and David Perkins provide the answer: Because the world is changing rapidly, a change that we cannot stop and which brings dilemmas about globalisation, new technologies and educational abilities to keep up with the process (see Chemi, 2009e).

Today's pupils need competencies that they can use in a technologically advanced world: "Kids are reinventing civilization: How do we help them?" (Dede in Chemi, 2009e, p. 47). Art forms like film and animation, electronic music, etc., art forms that use technological means, which advantageously can be included in a curriculum for tomorrow's schools. At the same time, technical and practical tools from more traditional forms of art are used to create the necessary cognitive competencies for the future: Visual understanding and interpretation, creative new thinking and an approach to learning, etc.

Unfortunately, none of the interviewed pupils named anything about professional competency or learning acquired from the aesthetic or art-oriented tools such as composition, function, function of an artwork. This comprehension, which is probably perceived as part of the theoretical subject's domain, remained separated from the pupils' involvement in a practical artistic creative process.

Mindset

The outcome of the different development projects are also characterised by a more intangible area: The mindset, i.e. the cognitive procedures or processes that the pupils take to heart. I define mindset as a way of thinking or a specific way of thinking that can open the way for preferred ways of thinking or dispositions if they are practised systematically over a longer period of time. The preferred ways of thinking or dispositions are linked here with the cognitive learning theories about "thinking dispositions" (Perkins, 1992a; 1992b and 2009).

"I've learned what I needed to learn" is at first sight a superficial statement but what lies behind the comment is a displayed flexibility in the use of the tools the pupils have learned to use (see above and subsequent quotes from the Nørup School pupils' interviews). What the child means is: "I have learned what I needed to learn to solve the task in the given situation and context," or "I have learned what the school expects of me". To learn to use a mindset can affect one's own learning in a positive form of learning habits or patterns. For example, a mindset can affect social behaviour, "I have learned to collaborate with others in a group" or the methodological: I have learned that "if I try it again, it'll probably be better", "I have learned that it takes time to make a short film. And you can make a film with just a few things", "I have learned that some things take a long time to make" (Chemi, 2011, p. 68). The awareness of technical methods and tools that some of the pupils show, for example at Nørup School, turns learning towards a craftsmanship way of thinking, i.e. they understand how an animation artists thinks in practice: To put a short film together takes a long time, you need to try several times and practice before you get better at craftsmanship, you can find inspiration or a good story using very few things. If you cultivate this thinking, the pupils will have an artistic (or artful) approach to learning by establishing a preferred way of thinking.

At Andkær School, the influence of the participating professional artist was also very clear in the pupils' interviews. With very little effort, the pupils point out the "professional" quality in Peitersen's approach to the work of art: "Compared to when we have to draw or paint the pictures ourselves, it's something else when a professional does them", "He tells it in another way and said some other things and stuff, different from when our teachers say it when we shall paint". In their eyes, Peitersen's approach is clearly professional and different from when they do it on their own or in school. A professional artist does things differently, talks differently and you can learn by it. Peitersen's influence has affected a large part of the children's learning or the children's perception of their own learning, which was also confirmed in the interview with the educators in the coordination group: "[Peitersen] got [the pupils] to think" (ibid.).

Some statements from Andkær School pupils show a deeper understanding of the way professional artists think, which is the result of the pupils' exposure to the participating painter's thinking. These statements have almost a poetic quality, which makes them difficult to decode, for example: "[I have learned that] it doesn't always have to be easy, and sometimes you have to work hard and try even when you're maybe not so good at it"; "[I have learned that] art doesn't always have to be straight and exact. It can be very different", "I have learned that you must not stop because the picture stops, it has to look as if you're moving on. Just because the picture stops, the drawing doesn't stop", "It doesn't have to be exact and stop when it stops", "I understand anyway why [the artists] love to paint" (ibid.). What the children are trying to say here is that even though you make an effort, in the world of art, when it comes to the creation of art, a good result is a matter of perspective. There are different ways to paint and technical precision is not necessarily that which makes a picture good or expressive. Unfortunately, these reflections have not been supported by a debate where the teachers could set a cultural, artistic and professional perspective on the children's insights. For example, it would have been effective for the children's understanding if their impressions were corroborated, that yes quite rightly, in the world of art, technical perfection is not always that which is the most expressive, charming, meaningful and cause of wonder. These children have captured the process quality in the creation of art (a process that never stops), but the learning was not "harvested" during the project week because the course was designed with a practical focus that pushed aside and excluded the reflective part.

Teachers' own cognitive challenges

Just like their pupils, teachers and kindergarten teachers are challenged on the cognitive and intellectual level when they get involved in development projects with art. First and foremost, these projects and the meeting with art and artists require that the teachers invent their own model. There is nothing in the curriculum they can use, there is no manual that can help them. All of the art forms are different and can be used in many different ways. All of the artists are different and a collaboration with them requires a certain amount of restructuring of uniform teaching. This results in the teachers becoming creative and inventive.

The many dilemmas, as the teachers at Nørup School put it, are a million miles from sheer uncertainty, rather it is a sign of the many positive considerations. These teachers show that they do not take teaching for granted and are willing to rethink their teaching style and forms.

These dilemmas, visualised in Figure 3 Teachers' and artists' answers, Nørup School, are both about practical considerations about how educators can specifically integrate animation in the classroom teaching but also more general themes about how the pupils acquire the learning they must learn and how they do it.

The metareflection that these teachers show is very diverse among the participating schools but the trend is that the schools that cultivate the aesthetic learning processes in general, appear to be more reflective than the schools that only engage with artistic activity in a limited project form. U School had even developed their own theoretical model based on Austrin & Sørensen (2006, p. 75) and in the focus group interview, the participating teachers show a high level of theoretical awareness. Nevertheless, the gap between theory and practice is difficult to bridge. Many of U School's teachers know hardly anything about the theoretical model, which is a sign that the model is not integrated into the school's practices.

The teachers in the Artfulness study have a clear picture of their pupils' cognitive development in the artistic projects. Even though they do not carry out systematically ad-hoc evaluations, the teachers have a clear feeling that the pupils have developed and how. By evaluation, I do not mean a standard text or exam but a joint reflection shared together with the children and focused on the teaching development (evaluation *for* teaching and learning rather than an evaluation *of* the teaching and learning).

These teachers emphasise the following cognitive outcome for the children's intellectual challenges:

- Tolerance and collaboration
  The children accept each other's differences and different ways of thinking and acting, which means that they develop a positive *team spirit*. All of the pupils who have had projects where they collaborated with others, show a greater disposition to helping each other, across classes, age groups and genders. The project form or whole school projects as frameworks that facilitate the meeting between the individual and the collegial learning: Children use each other to realise their own individual ideas and establish a constructive cooperation in groups.

- Positive feedback
  Children are disposed to positive challenging and appreciative feedback. For example, the teachers on the KDH (art, design, crafts)

course at Engum School did not experience the children acting in a condescending way, or any of them teasing or ridiculing others.

- Creativity
  Several teachers and educators praised the children's ability to be creative and to think new. The pupils appear to have learned that in art, there is always the possibility of re-doing something if it does not work.

- Quality awareness
  The pupils from Nørup School for example, show a sense for detail, pride in the work and an awareness of quality in relation to the product they are creating. The pupils from Andkær School have a special approach to learning, a seriousness and dedication (commitment) which raises the level of quality awareness. When I challenged their understanding of the artistic "stains" and asked them, a little provocatively, if they had the urge to paint outside of the lines because it was neither here nor there, they answered contemplatively: "Why should we do that?" (Chemi, 2010b). Quite rightly, why should a child compromise on quality with a task that he or she finds meaningful and energy-giving? The child will not.

- Understanding of the medium
  The teachers from Nørup School for example, believe that their pupils have learned animation as a medium so much so that they have also learned to trust in the media and the process and believe that the result will be attractive no matter what. This finding agrees well with the other literature and media in teaching (see Gardner & Davies, 2013).

Art experiences and learning

To summarise, I will emphasise the special relationship that emotions and cognition have in a learning perspective within art experiences. Every artwork is a complex jigsaw puzzle, which the players (the observers, listeners, readers and recipients) must put together in their own personal way. The results from this combination represents a mix of personal choices, which are based on an individual's psychological, social, cultural, emotional and biological background. The art inspires these emotional and cognitive processes using many different functions, such as (Chemi, 2012a):

- Complexity: The artworks are often created by challenging several senses, emotions and thoughts at the same time.
- Opacity: The art never directly reflects the real world. It hides, conceals and covers: The recipients' and the makers' work consists of uncovering, finding and recognising the hidden meanings.
- Metaphors: The artworks are built on metaphors and generate metaphorical mental images.
- Communication in absentia: Art communicates with what it shows and what it hides. For example, pauses in drama or music are just as important as lines and tones.
- Sensory and physical qualities: The artworks are created in the present moment through sensory and physical materials and media.
- Meaningfulness: "form and content is a false division derived from another false division, thought and feeling" (Judd, 2003, p. 1142), therefore the artworks are always both form and content, so that they create meaning and meaningful associations or relationships.
- Social dimension: The art is shared by and with people.

The arts build a complex environment and system of meanings, which must be decoded. This means a network of meanings is created, where at the same time complex (and therefore challenging) activities and safe frameworks are found, therefore art is prone to generate positive emotions. To learn in and through art can be experienced as "safe" because the art gives us an extraordinary experience, i.e. an experience that is simultaneously part of our real world and different from ordinary everyday life. These learning environments are safe because they belong to the world of the imagination and of symbols (Langer, 1953), where it is allowed to be different, to be another person, to be provocative and extreme. Experience in art is safe because despite the intensive emotional involvement, it still belongs to an extraordinary dimension. Lévi-Strauss (1969) says that our feeling of safety is just an illusion of having control of a chaotic field but nevertheless the art is able to give us a - good and safe -feeling, thus we can make sense, and therefore we can understand the world.

The Artfulness study interviews and observations show that the participants experience a strong drive in a task, which is motivated from within and often *autotelic* (having a purpose in and not apart from itself). This strong motivation is not rare in art experiences, if we understand inner motivation (as in Goleman, 2006) as stimulation of: Autonomy in the task, ownership, competency in appreciation and the cognitive application of skills. Art offers a broad range of independence in the interpretation of artworks, expression and translation of artworks. Finally, the principle of ownership is specific for the creation of art.

Elliot Eisner (1991) maintains that what is unique about art is that it gives expression to meanings, which are often non-literal (representative symbols). In contrast to scientific symbols, which point at the meanings which they are intended to convey and which refer to their transparency, the artistic symbols are opaque (Eisner, 1991, p. 31). The opacity of art characterises all forms of artistic artefacts, even the most realistic. Artworks are constructed using a systematic and programmatic strategy of concealing and obscuring, which is both irrelevant and contradictory to other epistemic traditions such as science. Science is required to explicate and communicate as clearly as possible, art hides its meanings, objectives, tools, processes, etc., to express through complexity and to express complexity. Even cultural attempts to show "what is hidden" in the art repeats this artistic guise. These elements of artistic form, complex texts with many levels and opacity are themselves the core of the artistic dialectics. According to David Perkins, art is invisible and "the invisibility of art is virtually a logical consequence of how art functions as a symbol system" (1994, p. 21). The concept is advocated by Goodman (1976), who expresses art's density as *repleteness*, but it can be traced back to other theorists too (Murray, 2003). It is paradoxical that art's "invisibility" appears to contradict the other specific qualities of art, based on materiality, physicality and mediation. Artworks are artefacts, things that are visible and experienced though the senses. Despite this, "it's not the work that is invisible but our way of looking at it that fails to make it visible" (Perkins, 1994, p.

32). The cognitive work we are asked to carry out in the art is to perceive and understand what is anticipated, and what is hidden. What is anticipated is the object of perception and decoding.

The artists' strategies are for the most part hidden, the art's objectives, meanings and messages are disseminated with the help of dense symbols, metaphors and allegories, which make the perception and understanding of the artwork a complex task of decoding man-made artefacts. Often art is expressed *in absentia*, that is the absence of colours, sound, movements, etc. The cognitive enigmas that are offered within art force us to interrupt the rhythm of our thinking and to turn our attention towards a deep understanding and reflection. The reason that artworks are meaningful and create meanings, regardless of which form they take or the content that they disseminate, either as fully-formed or fragmentary or incomprehensible, abstract or absent materials.

Therefore, despite there being many different activities in addition to art that generate positive feedback or which challenge individuals cognitively or which generate flow experiences, artworks seem to be systematically devised and designed for the purpose of creating positive emotions (in an Aristotelian sense) and flow experiences. Artworks provide a learning environment with many learning opportunities. The role of educators is to fully exploit these opportunities in their own contexts and in meaningful ways.

Art can systematically stimulate positive emotions, for example joy (which interviewed participants in the Artfulness study reported), which can lead to a short-term urge to play and a long-term development of the physical, intellectual and social skills that individuals require for learning (for the connection between learning and positive emotions, see Fredrickson 1998, pp. 304-306). When participants in the Artfulness project reported an increased interest either for the academic subject conveyed by art or in their newly discovered artistic competencies, this might lead to a short-term urge to explore and to a long-term accumulation of knowledge. In both cases, the interviewees reported both a strong desire to learn, play with or explore the art forms that they experienced in the project, and a deep acquired knowledge, which they described as different and more enjoyable than ordinary learning in the school.

Finally, there is only one wish that I want to express: On the basis of the wide theoretical support and empirical evidence for art's central role in learning and well-being related to learning, I would like to see a more serious and systematic inclusion of art in formal learning environments and its integration with the academic, logical and scientific learning. My hope is that the next part of the book will provide many opportunities for inspiration and concrete, practicable tools for this purpose.

How do we achieve it

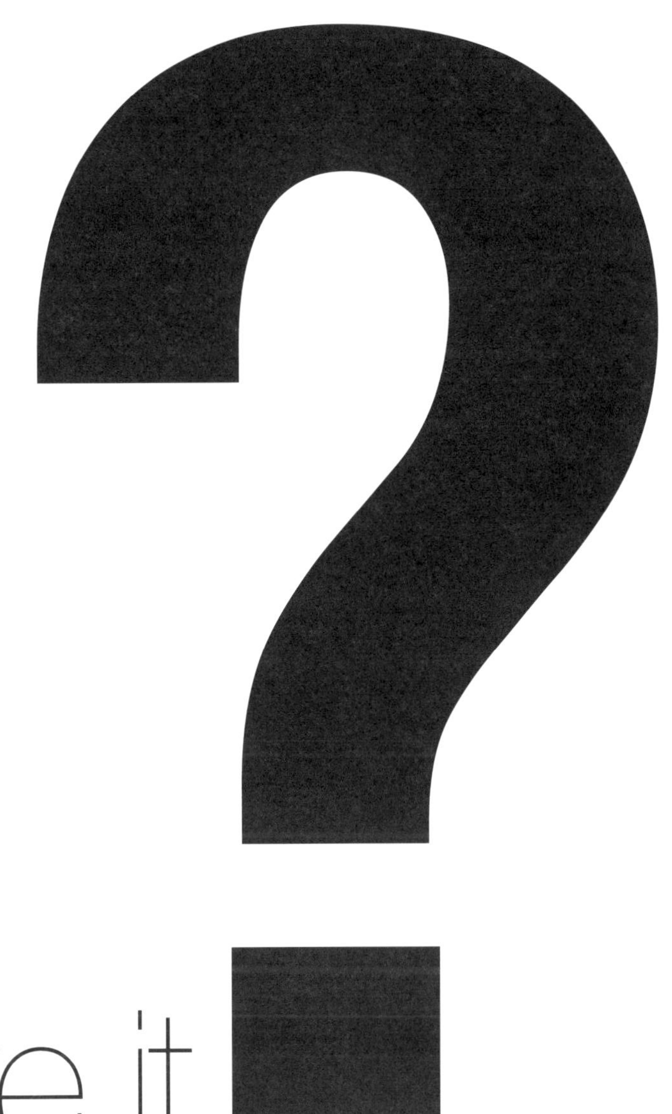

Part two

How to integrate the arts in education

For many years in Denmark and in Scandinavia in general, schools have cultivated a tradition for project work and taken a cross-disciplinary approach to teaching. Unfortunately, this tradition is being challenged by the many pressing requirements for attaining improved PISA results. This is a contradictory process in relation to what is defined in the literature as *Progressive Education*, a pedagogic direction inspired by Dewey, Bruner, Gardner, Malaguzzi and others.

Even though there are several examples in Denmark of progressive school practice and the present book is based on Danish cases, I wish to report on a case from the USA that concerns a form of teaching that is based on group work, cross-disciplinary collaboration, integration of creative subjects throughout the curriculum, meaningful learning tasks and more. Expeditionary Learning is a term that refers both to a network of schools and to an educational approach. The Expeditionary Learning network consists of about 150 schools, which are spread across the whole of the USA and which share the same ideals, school structure and specific educational tools. These schools are often a type known as "charter schools", i.e. schools with special bylaws and with a specific and often progressive learning vision.

As an educational approach, Expeditionary Learning (Berger, 2003) and the Reggio Emilia schools in Italy (Vecchi, 2010) are examples of practices that come closest to an artful ideal. These examples show that a complete revolution of the school timetable and school routines is possible and fruitful. I will describe this approach, so that it will inspire other teachers in the belief that what they dream of, can be accomplished.

Expeditionary Learning can be directly compared to *experiential learning*, i.e. learning based on experience. In Expeditionary Learning schools, teaching is structured as an expedition, i.e. a thematic journey where the pupils become actively involved, in accordance with certain principles:

Project-based: The teaching is planned as coherent projects or expeditions.

Arts-*infused*: Different art forms are integrated throughout the curriculum and in all of the subjects and disciplines.

Cross-disciplinary: All of the subjects contribute to the expedition theme and specific focus.

Group-based: The pupils work in groups and the groups are made up of pupils of different genders and ages.

Excellence: The overall (artful) ideal is "excellence", i.e. focusing attention on quality. Ron Berger, a leading expert in and practitioner of Expeditionary Learning, uses craftsmanship as a metaphor:

> "In the classroom or on the building site my passion is the same: If you're going to do something, I believe, you should do it well. You should sweat over it and make sure it's strong and accurate and beautiful and you should be proud of it. In carpentry there is no higher compliment builders give to each other than this: That guy is a craftsman. This one word says it all. It connects someone who has integrity and knowledge, who is dedicated to his work and who is proud of what he does and who he is. Someone who thinks carefully and does things well.
> I want a classroom full of craftsmen. I want students whose work is strong and accurate and beautiful. Students who are proud of what they do, proud of how they respect both themselves and others" (Berger, 2003, p. 1).

The focus on quality is cultivated in the following areas and in the following ways:

- Use of (excellent) materials: The children are almost instinctively aware of quality, they can recognise quality and they are affected by the material's sensory quality. If they work with high-quality materials, their quality awareness will become heightened.
- Models and expert advice: Both older students at the school and experts inspire and guide the pupils along their learning expedition. Examples of older or previous pupils' work are used as

models, sources of inspiration and prototypes. By presenting the pupils with diverse solutions, they are encouraged not to blindly follow a single model. In addition, the pupils look at the end product and the many prototypes or draft versions that they created along the way to realising their final version. In this way, the models inspire the pupils to find original solutions and not just to make carbon copies. When external models are used, it is a more a case of providing expert advice. The schools invite experts to visit and give a talk or to inspect the quality of the work. These experts are introduced to the school's pedagogic approach and values by the pupils and this means that the expert can give appreciative and positive feedback (positive response). In this way, the school creates positive peer-pressure, i.e. the pupils become motivated in wanting to perform as well as or better than the older pupils or experts.

- Draft culture: The pupils have the opportunity to re-work their work several times. The different versions are saved for the purpose of documenting the process and for enabling the pupils to reflect on mistakes and optimal solutions. Mistakes are viewed as unique learning opportunities and time is frequently set aside for their closer examination. The pupils do not feel ashamed about their mistakes, because they know a mistake is just part of a broader and longer process: A process where criticism does not stop activities dead in their tracks but instead initiates a rewarding and energetic learning process. This is achieved among other things, by using the pupils' portfolio as an active tool during the learning process and during teaching. The pupils' portfolio is viewed as a means to make learning visible, i.e. it is used as process documentation, showing both the strengths and requirements (for more about portfolio, see Seldin, 2004).
- Pupil performance/dissemination: The majority of learning expeditions are used for "serious" learning, i.e. the pupils write and publish real books, draw and print real postcards, carry out real geological measurements. The majority of these activities also have a practical use: The books and postcards are sold, the measurements are submitted to the local town council. Income

Race to Nowhere is an American documentary film that shows the emotional and psychological consequences of an education system that pressurises children and young people with unsuitable testing and requirements.
For more details about the documentary film, visit www.racetonowhere.com.

More details about Expeditionary Learning schools

http://elschools.org/
www.edutopia.org/passion-knowledge-introduction-expeditionary-learning

is used to finance the purchasing of expensive, high-quality educational materials. The pupils' performance, i.e. dissemination of their learning tasks has a crucial function – to make the learning and understanding that has been achieved visible and meaningful to everyone. However, there is some risk that product-oriented teaching in the schools is perceived as performance-oriented pressure on results and blind assessment. A pressure on the teachers and pupils that must be weighed up and measured and which has been shown to be stressful and unrewarding, if not downright damaging: "[pressure for expectations and constant testing] encourages a perfectionist tendency and encourages individuals to put unrealistic pressure on themselves" (Robinson, 2001, p. 52).

To avoid a "teach to the test" logic, it is therefore crucial that the right conditions are created for active participation in the learning process and thus ensure the optimal nurturing of creativity. Research and Expeditionary Learning practice shows that a targeted effort in a specific work or performance ensures that the pupils get the prerequisites for optimal learning:

- Clear frameworks for the development process.
- Concrete and meaningful challenges.
- Tangible success experiences and feedback.

Within Expeditionary Learning for example, the pupils' "performances" in the form of a concrete product, are an organic part of the teaching process and the pupils' learning process. In this regard, the aesthetic subjects prove themselves to be a crucial training ground for concentration and a reservoir of creative resources. Expeditionary Learning, with its "arts-infused" curriculum, like Anne Bamford's "art-rich" schools and similar concepts for high-quality aesthetic experiences in the learning framework, describes the same trend I have observed at Engum School (Chemi, 2009b). The children love challenges, they want to solve the difficult problems and clear frameworks can facilitate their task even more, if they can see a purpose. "To worry is to care about performance: give them a reason to care and do the job optimally" (from Berger, 2003, p. 99).

David Perkins (2009) recommends a "junior version" of teaching, which is exactly what was observed in for example, the architect project at Engum School: The children learn to "play" with reality on genuine terms and with a concrete task. They come to understand the rules for everyday life and for their family's choices when it comes to the family home and to daily finances.

"Our real criterion of understanding has to be performance. People understand something when they can think and act flexibly with what they know about it, not just rehearse information and execute routine skills. If you can't think with Newton's laws, you don't really understand them. If you can't think and act like a citizen, you don't really understand what citizenship is all about" (Perkins, 2009, p. 49).

This short account introduces the possibility of integrating art in teaching in a whole-school dimension. This perspective is possible, desirable and rewarding, which the major successes from for example, Expeditionary Learning schools demonstrate.

Creativity

Regardless of which project the teacher initiates with help from artistic tools and processes, it will be appropriate if creativity is also introduced as a subject that the class can reflect on. Teachers who are interested in stimulating the pupils' creative potential, will find it advantageous if they make this objective clear to their pupils. This will allow the pupils to reflect upon their own creativity, the importance of creativity in their lives and in the history of humanity and its development. This reflection can usefully pave the way for a creative activity and strengthen the activity's creative output, for the simple reason that

Thinking disposition

The concept "Thinking disposition", consists of four cognitive actions: Awareness of the learning material, motivation for learning, inclination for learning, learning abilities (Ritchhart, 2002).

the pupils are more aware of and more focused on, what creativity means. The more an individual knows about creativity and its processes, the more he or she is inclined to use this knowledge to acquire new knowledge in the area. If creativity training is systematic and long-term, a creative response can become a disposition, i.e. a thinking disposition.

The reader should be aware that this view of the creative response, which is strongly linked to the knowledge of and training in creativity, is not necessarily in opposition to the "spontaneous" view of creativity. Some believe that creativity is purely a spontaneous process and that any awareness about its processes, tools and effects will prevent an optimal creative development. It is my belief that the two things are complementary. On the one hand, it goes without saying that the more LEGO bricks someone has the bigger the house they can build, but on the other hand, spending too many hours putting LEGO bricks together may mean some people fail to see new possibilities. Our creative competencies function in the same way: Knowledge (LEGO bricks) is necessary for creation (the house), but expertise can blind us to new possibilities. Creativity is built on a routine disposition for creative thinking (expertise) and a sustained naivety (spontaneity). However, Ellen Langer (2006) shifts the focus to the approach that the individual acquires within the creative processes: According to the American researcher, creativity occurs when a person is completely mindful, i.e. they are in the moment and attentive (Langer, 1993, 1997, 2003). In my opinion, artistic creativity needs both expertise and fresh perspectives, which can be cultivated by being in the moment and never taking expertise or spontaneity for granted.

In the schools or in informal learning environments, it is possible to cultivate this approach and to stimulate creativity optimally. The following reflection guide is highly recommended for anyone who is initiating a learning process with focus on creativity. In addition, while the practical creative activity is underway, the open questions in this guide can be very useful aids for also maintaining focus on the reflective part.

Reflection guide for creative learning processes

Objective: To stimulate the pupils' new thinking and sense of realism.

Preparation: The teachers bring together several definitions of creativity, new thinking and innovation (Google, Wikipedia, Kaufman & Sternberg, 2010).

Start-up: The pupils are introduced to the language of creativity through brainstorming of the following:

- What does creativity mean?
- When have you created something that is "creative"? How do you know?
- When have you gotten a good/new idea? How do you know?
- If an idea is good and new, what should it consist of?
- What does new thinking mean?
- What does innovation mean?

NB: When this brainstorming session is underway, it is important that it is the pupils who answer the questions. Teachers should not be afraid of silence. If the children are silent, it does not mean that time is being wasted in the class. Teachers should prepare the pupils in how long they have to reflect on the questions or on an individual question. For example: You have two minutes to think about it on your own and five minutes to share your thoughts with the person next to you. The teacher can support and stimulate the pupils' curiosity, either by proposing potential answers to the pupils' questions or by helping the children to describe what they are curious about. Finally, the teacher should allow the children to express their own wonder.

Documentation: When the pupils brainstorm, a visualisation of the reflections will help the process. This can either take place on the board, a flip chart, on a smart board or on large sheets of paper, where the pupils write or sketch their answers. Finally, teachers should give the pupils the opportunity to be physically active and allow them to come up to the board/smart board/flip chart and write down or sketch their ideas. The children's favourite post-its can be stuck to foreheads, the wall, chairs, etc. Post-its are ideal because they can be grouped in accordance with themes, for example if several children answer that creativity means to paint, all of the similar answers can be grouped under "to create". The following is an example of how the children's potential answers to "what is creativity" could be grouped:

To think
To get ideas
To have imagination
To think differently

To create
To paint
To make bead necklaces
To sing well

To Play
To play with materials
To have fun
To move

The key words here indicate a categorisation of creativity as "something you do by creating something" or "something you think" or "something playful". By grouping the pupils' answers, the teacher categorises them, which immediately invites metareflection (reflection upon reflection). The teacher can and should encourage the pupils to understand the blue categories. This cognitive exercise stimulates the children's analogical thinking, i.e. the ability to see analogies and similarities.

This brainstorming is based on a shared language regarding creativity and a shared understanding of creativity's many faces, which will be expressed in the practical phase of the creative-artistic activity.

Design

In 2009, the Danish Ministry of Education issued a press release called "Creative Subjects become examination subjects as a trial" (my translation), for the purpose of publicising its renewed interest for the aesthetic subjects in education (Danish Ministry of Education, 2009). Another focus in the Danish Ministry of Education's press release was its recommendation for the merging of needlework, handicrafts (incl. woodwork), and even art, into a single subject: "*Handicrafts and Design* will be a trial offer and will become an examination subject. *Handicrafts and Design* is a new subject which will replace needlework, handicrafts (incl. woodwork) and eventually, art" (ibid., my translation from the Danish). This new subject is often referred to as "Design". Subsequently, 24 trials of the subject were initiated across the country during the school year 2010-2011. But already prior to this in the school year 2008-2009, a major trial was initiated at Engum School in Vejle Municipality (Chemi, 2009b). The following practical examples of the teaching process in design are either directly reported from that trial or are ideas inspired by the project.

What makes you say that?

Exercise in promoting the ability to support an assertion with evidence.

What happens in the picture?
What is it that you see, which gets you to interpret the picture in that way?

WHICH WAYS OF THINKING ASSIST THIS EXERCISE?

This exercise helps learners to describe what they see or what they know and to become even better at constructing arguments. This helps evidence-based argumentation, and because the exercise encourages learners to share their interpretations with others, it can enhance their ability to see other alternatives and different perspectives. The person learns to separate interpretations and reasoning.

WHEN AND WHERE CAN IT BE USED?

Because the basic questions in this exercise are very flexible, they are useful for example, when examining art or historical artefacts. They can also be used to interpret poetry, in more or less scientific observations and hypotheses, in the study of concepts (e.g. democracy). This exercise can be used by almost anyone and can also be useful in mapping the pupils' knowledge about a subject before a new topic is introduced.

(Adapted from Visible Thinking, 2009)

Main theme: Architecture

WARM UP: Reflection on creativity (using the above guide) and presentation of very different architectural styles. The teachers can use the internet to collect different pictures for a slide show or loan books about architecture from the library. The important thing is that the pictures that are shown to the children are attractive, engaging and works of high quality, and that they demonstrate a wide diversity of styles. The teachers can supplement this presentation by asking the pupils open questions for the purpose of stimulating a dialogue about architecture's many dimensions. The exercises in the green boxes may be used for inspiration: "I see, I think, I wonder," and "What makes you say that?"

The teachers should remember to link an assertion or opinion with a specific observation based on the pictures that are shown. Remember to always return to the picture and ask the pupils to point out the named details or observations.

I see, I think, I wonder

This exercise helps develop the ability to observe, reflect and ask questions.

What do you see in the picture?
What do you think about this picture?
Is there something in this picture that you wonder about?

WHICH WAYS OF THINKING ASSIST THIS EXERCISE?

This exercise helps the learners to describe what they see or what they know and to become even better at constructing questions around an argument. This helps evidence-based argumentation, and because the exercise encourages learners to share their interpretations with others, it can enhance their ability to see other alternatives and different perspectives. The person learns to separate observations, personal reflections and puzzlement.

WHEN AND WHERE CAN IT BE USED?

Because the basic questions in this exercise are very flexible, they can be used in many contexts, particularly when the person looks at for example, art, images, historical artefacts or other visual material. This exercise can be used by almost anyone and can also be useful in mapping the pupils' knowledge about a subject before a new subject is introduced.

(Adapted from Visible Thinking, 2009)

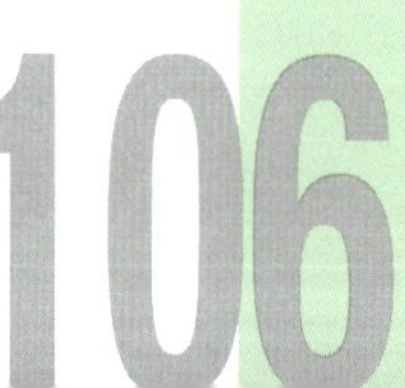

TASKS: The teacher can choose one of these practical tasks:

1. To plan and build a house for a family. This task can start with a short exercise in constructing a story, where the pupils are asked to imagine a family and then to build a house for that family. This exercise in fiction can be more or less complex or it can be integrated in an academic subject. For example, the story can be written (Danish, English or some other language), dramatised (drama, dance) or visualised (art, digital media). Or the teachers can choose that this family comes from a specific historical period (history) or geographical area (geography).

2. When this background material is finished, the task's handicraft phase can begin.

3. To design a building with specific functions, for example a school, a swimming pool, a football stadium. This task should begin with an examination of functionality as an element in artefacts and can be used to introduce a connection with the natural sciences (nature and technology, physics, biology).

4. To design a fantasy building. This task is the one that most stimulates the imagination and new thinking. For the purpose of inviting the pupils into a space where they imagine something they have no knowledge of, the teachers will have to work a little longer with radical brainstorming. The teachers should encourage crazy thinking and provoke the pupils using humour and with a serious appreciation of mistakes.

Radical brainstorming

Stimulates the pupils using unusual sensory input, e.g. by listening to unusual music (Klezmer, world music, ethnic or electronic music is recommended), by moving around a room in an unfamiliar way (unusual, grotesque and funny movements are recommend), by tasting exotic fruit or foods and describing their taste.

Some ideas for tasks in sensory exercises:

Find opposites in visual, auditory or taste-related exercises, for example white/black, round/square, sweet/sour.

Associate images and taste in a story, for example sour/sunset.

Find a metaphor, for example "a house is a rose".

Create bold associations in narratives.

5. To design or mimic a building with a specific theme, for example Star Wars or Jumanji or World of War Craft (all depending on age, since there are age limits) or the Muppet Show as the main themes. In this task, the teacher should let the children choose their favourites and encourage them to use the fantasy world that they like the most. The teacher can expect a high degree of engagement from the pupils, which should be cultivated and maintained.

DESIGN/HANDICRAFT: When the pupils shall build a prototype for their work, there will be several options available. Depending on the cross-disciplinary collaboration that the teachers will establish, the pupils may be asked:

1. To draw a plan of the house/building. This model invites a collaboration with mathematics and an inclusion of mathematics and geometry tasks. Measurements, proportions, calculations, geometric figures and formulas and trigonometry are just some of the competencies the pupils can practice while they draw their house. Because the pupils better remember what they learn when they have a use for it, it will be helpful if the mathematical instruments are introduced on an ongoing basis. The teachers do not need to separate the theoretical part (learning of mathematical principles) and the practical part (application of the mathematical principles). This task invites the inclusion of the humanities, if the teachers choose to introduce this task by preparatory work, where the pupils describe the family that will live in the house (written descriptions, reading the background material about the family's archetypes, etc.).

2. To build a model of the house/building. This model introduces a collaboration using mathematics and the practical subjects like woodwork and other handicrafts, and art. Even though this model requires a more intuitive and free approach to the design task, the teachers can encourage the pupils to use their mathematical knowledge for the purpose of solving the task (creative problem solving supported by school subjects). The collaboration between the creative subjects requires that the teachers coordinate

the individual knowledge and find their unique way of integrating them. The teachers in the three design subjects at Engum School in Vejle (Chemi, 2009b) agreed to combine their teaching hours so that the pupils could carry out cross-disciplinary work on a design project for one whole day a week. The three teachers prepared both the activities and the approach in a collaboration, and as a group, they received advice from a creativity expert. This meant that they achieved a shared understanding of the overall objectives and for the practical activities that they had to initiate. This model focuses on the handicraft and sensory materials perspective, and therefore it is important for the teachers to emphasise this by examining different materials, their function and their properties.

3. To draw and subsequently build a model. This model integrates the two models named above and has a unique advantage: The teachers can stimulate a "draft culture" in the classroom to a greater extent. The two tasks, which build on each other, give rise to minutely detailed work. The transfer of the drawing to a three-dimensional prototype can both include academic subjects (two-dimensional vs three-dimensional geometry) and methodological approaches such as quality awareness, positive response, feedback sessions and more.

EXPERT VISIT: It is recommended that the teachers' lessons are supplemented with a visit by an expert in the area; an architect who can provide instruction, supervision and advice for the pupils' work. To get an optimal output, the expert should be invited in the middle of the process, when the pupils have the opportunity to actively use the expert's feedback and good advice in the work. To invite an expert at the end of the process will give the pupils a feeling of being in an exam with an external examiner and they will not have the opportunity to benefit from what they learn during the meeting. The expert should be prepared for the task and be informed about the basic pedagogic principles of appreciative feedback and positive response. It is recommended that the pupils take care of this task, under the prerequisite that the rules for good feedback are laid down as a group and that the pupils are properly prepared for the task. It is also recommended that everyone strictly follows the schedule. The children can help to devise and execute the schedule, so that all of the children and all of the project groups have the same conditions and opportunities to get feedback from the expert. Ethnographic research about the inclusion of experts in teaching shows that the pupils experience a high degree of frustration if the expert does not manage to take all of the children's work into account (ibid.).

ON-GOING EVALUATION: For the purpose of strengthening the learning experience, an evaluation is required. All of the learning individuals need direct feedback, i.e. they need to know how well they are doing and that they can do something if something is not working. Ensuring that there is an evaluation that focuses on this, will be energising and *empowering* and at the same time it will strengthen the learning process. An evaluation for learning and not of learning can be achieved by for example, a feedback session where both the pupils and teachers respond positively to one another. When working with cultural artefacts (art or design or more general artefacts), it can be helpful to always refer to a specific and visible "thing". During evaluations, this may help promote an understanding of any criticism that is expressed and help to visualise its evidence. Specifically, the pupils' works can visualise their learning process and help the teachers and the pupils correct anything that is not working optimally. A feedback session that for example, takes its inspiration from artistic studios (or workshops) will function in the following way:

- The works are visualised and displayed for everyone.
- The pupils give polite but challenging feedback to each other.
- Focus on appreciation ("I see you") and evidence (point at something specific on the work).
- Focus on feedback, which can be used to improve the work (a response like "this work is ugly" cannot be used positively but "this part of the work does not work because...." can help to initiate good reflections).
- Focus on non-patronising discussion.

- The pupils ask each other open questions and focus on the work ("How/why/what did you do ...?").
- The pupils offer proposals to how the work can be improved ("Have you thought about ......?")

CONCLUSION: A good conclusion should be meaningful, useful and "genuine". Many of the school projects that the pupils are engaged in, begin and end in the school. This inherent logic results in a closed approach to learning, where learning does not extend beyond the school's domain.

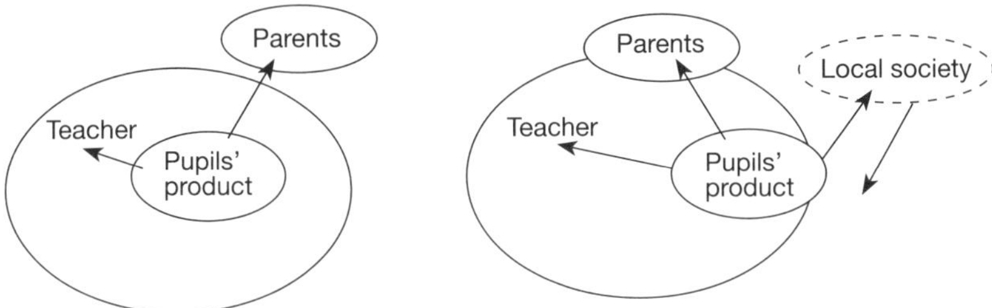

Figure 8 Who appreciates the students' artworks?

The above figure (Chemi, 2009b, p. 52) shows two approaches to the pupils' artworks, i.e. the specific products of their learning process. The first on the left shows the current general approach: The pupils create artworks that their teachers, or at best, parents experience within the closed environment of school. The desirable model is the one on the right, where the parents collaborate more closely with the school and where the pupils' artworks are experienced by people outside of the school. A public showing of the results in a location that is outside the school can be systematically cultivated to advantage, using the awareness that a good, complete, quality-conscious work process will be shown with pride. This creates positive feelings of co-ownership and accomplishment in the children and at the same time creates good evaluation material for the teachers, not just based on academic presentation but on the children's deep understanding and learning.

In the case of a design initiative that focuses on architecture, a public display of the children's artworks can be celebrated with the involvement of their parents or in collaboration with local architects, designers or entrepreneurs who are experts in their field.

An example of a good case

The following is an example of a complete project (a fictitious example but one which is inspired by an actual project):

Three teachers at X School have decided to enter into a cross-disciplinary collaboration in mathematics, art/design and English in their joint grade five class. The three teachers prepare by reading different articles about creativity and creative techniques. They then exchange knowledge and opinions. Their sources are Google, Google Scholar, Kaufman & Sternberg, 2010, etc.

They choose to work with architecture as a theme. One of the teachers has a sister who is an architect and she can be involved in the process as an expert at no extra cost. One of the parents is a tradesman and may also be interested in contributing to the project. After this examination of the available resources, the teachers ask themselves the following:

- What do we want to achieve with this project?
    - Answer: We will generate a greater understanding of architectural procedures, architectural work and building regulations. At the same time, we will stimulate the pupils' critical sense and their creativity.

- What will the pupils learn and understand?
    - Answer: The pupils will learn to observe buildings and assess them on the basis of their materiality and aesthetic value. They will understand which things need to be considered when building a house. They will learn to appreciate the architect's way of thinking and creativity.

- Which meaningful activities should they become engaged in?
  - Answer: If our pupils are to find the tasks meaningful, we should either choose a fantasy world that they really like (toys, TV, youth culture) or a reality that they experience, such as a family home.

- Are the tasks that we choose engaging, meaningful, concretely and emotionally accessible or related to the pupils?
  - Answer: We teach pupils in fifth grade. They are used to searching for information on the internet, so they will easily find the necessary information. The task invites an emotional involvement.

- Can the tasks and themes invite a wide cross-disciplinary involvement?
  - Answer: With this task we can bring together mathematics, geometry, English, art, woodwork and other handicrafts (design).

The teachers consider which angle they will take and decide on a realistic approach, i.e. the pupils' task will be to create a prototype of a family home. The teachers are interested in stimulating both the pupils' creativity and sense of realism, so therefore they collect pictures of very different architectural styles. The sources are Google and architecture/design books.

As a warm-up to the project, the teachers and the pupils carry out a brainstorming session, examining what they think about creativity and innovation and what they know about building a house. Many of them live in houses that their parents have built or in older houses that their parents have renovated, so they will have some knowledge of building projects. The teachers run a slide show of their collection of pictures and encourage the pupils to carry out observation exercises (see the many examples above). The pupils record their contribution to the joint brainstorming session on yellow posit-its, which are categorised and transcribed in folders.

The pupils' first task takes place in groups, where they must think it over and devise a family or a group of people they want to build a house for. The children are encouraged to think out of the box and to

consider all of the many different ways people live together. The result is a great deal of diversity: A multi-ethnic group of friends, a rich and famous family with mum-dad-kids, a sports club only for boys, a family with a single mother and a small child, a family with several generations of family members or a family with same-sex parents. This task consists of a group interview, a written description and visual documentation in the form of drawings, sketches, collages, wax models or a mix of these. All of this material and other background information is collected in a folder (pupil portfolio).

When the groups have finished describing their "customers", they are given the task of making a plan drawing for a house for their fictive family. All of the groups are given a fixed budget, with a maximum amount. The teachers create some excitement about this: They have created cards with different amounts and the children must choose a card without being able to see the amount on it. The pupils use complex calculations, and check the costs of construction materials and furniture online. When they begin to draw the first version of their plan drawings, the mathematics teacher supplements the work with geometric and mathematical material.

When the drawings are finished, they are placed on the wall for a joint feedback session. Following the feedback session, the pupils are then allowed to redo their drawings and integrate the feedback they have received.

To facilitate the transfer of the drawn versions into a three-dimensional plan, the teachers have invited a professional architect to a feedback session. On arrival, the architect is welcomed by the pupils and given a short tour of the school. Among other things, the students tell the architect about the rules for feedback sessions that apply at their school. The architect gives a talk about her job and corrects the drawings by using professional terms and explaining them to the pupils.

The pupils have the opportunity to search for the new terms and their meanings and integrate the architect's proposals into their drawings.

The three-dimensional prototypes are built using wood board and various material (fabric, net, iron, natural wood, rubber, etc.) and by using the plan drawings. During the creation process, the pupils' learning is supported by on-going feedback sessions. The process is documented using photography.

When the models are close to being completed, the architect revisits the class. The architect's feedback is integrated into the models.

A public showing at the local library completes the project. Families, friends, associates, local residents and library users visit the library and examine the pupils' work.

Main theme: Picture frames

All of the general observations described above apply to this and the following tasks. A particular type of creativity is specifically used for this process: Product Development.

WARM UP: When starting a product development process, it is important that creative minds are warmed up. For this purpose, it can be beneficial to involve provocative techniques that point to other ways of thinking and acting. The teacher may find inspiration in play, drama/theatre, cooking, etc. See for example, the exercise in the text box "To explore creatively".

TASK: To build a picture frame that is different, from concept development to design. The task is introduced to the pupils by showing them several reproductions of different frames, from the internet, design books, furniture catalogues and fashion magazines. This process can be designed as a cross-disciplinary collaboration in art, woodwork/handicrafts, biol-

To explore creatively

This exercise is useful as a creative warm up, used by stage actors to stimulate their ability to associate. The exercise can be challenging and provocative. A short introduction to this task can be to allow the children to walk freely around the room at different paces and then as different kinds of people, e.g. as a tall person, fat person, prima donna, farmer or teenager. The actual task is about choosing one object and studying its many different functions by manipulating it and by arranging the different functions in the room. For example, a rope can be used as a tightrope, to hang in the air with, like spaghetti, as a chair, as a rope swing, etc. It is important that the participants use their entire body and not just think about it.

ogy, physics, and if required, mathematics, English and history. The design subjects contribute to among other things, the aesthetic dimension and the practical technical know-how. Biology can be incorporated by the use of natural materials (e.g. wood, fur, grass, leaves), physics and mathematics can be incorporated for challenging solutions and frames that inspire a mixed reaction, hanging materials or parts, untraditional geometric shapes, etc. The humanities subjects can be integrated if the teachers choose to limit the pupils' work to a specific historical period for inspiration, e.g. an Art Nouveau frame.

DESIGN/HANDICRAFT: The specific task can be free or themed, for example:

- Free development.
- The development of a different kind of picture frame using unusual materials or natural material or recycled materials or limiting the choice to just one kind of material, for instance metal.
- Development of inspiration from a specific historical/art historical period.
- Development of a theme from a fantasy world from children's culture, e.g. Mickey Mouse, the Smurfs, a particular children's book such as Harry Potter, etc.

EXPERT VISIT: It is recommended that the teacher uses a professional designer as their expert, because this person can give feedback regarding the artworks' aesthetic value and functionality. A student from a design school could coordinate this visit as a part of a practical assignment or as a study assignment. A good alternative could be to use a student from a teacher training college who is specialising in design (in Denmark for example, teacher training at University College Lillebælt is the first of its kind that has a line of study that focuses on material design).

CONTINUOUS FEEDBACK: Appreciative feedback should be developed on an on-going basis, so that the pupils have the opportunity to rework any picture frames that do not function optimally. The pupils should always have the opportunity to re-work any mistakes and to integrate feedback and proposals from the expert, the teachers and each other. NB: Appreciative feedback focuses not only on the positive elements or praise but also looks on mistakes as learning opportunities. This means that a mistake does not feel like a defeat, but rather something that the pupils can re-work. The important thing about an on-going evaluation process is the ability to provide and accept responses that can be used for something specific. This means that pupils should be allowed to address and assess what does not work in the artwork or artefact.

> You can't kick a ball against a curtain
>
> About positive response
> Boy, 13 years old (Bak, 2011)

CONCLUSION: Exhibition or sale of the picture frames at a school event or local event, such as a Christmas bazaar.

An example of a good case

The following is an example of a complete project (a fictitious example but which is inspired by an actual project):

Three teachers at Y School have decided to enter into a cross-disciplinary collaboration in biology, mathematics, art/design in their joint grade six class. The three teachers prepare by reading different articles about design and product development. They then exchange knowledge and opinions. Their sources are Google, Google Scholar and SlideShare.

They choose to work with picture frames as objects for creative product development. Their school is located close to a design school and the possibility of a collaboration can be considered and explored. After an examination of the available resources and allocation of tasks, they ask themselves the following:

- What do we want to achieve with this project?
  - Answer: We will generate a greater understanding of design and product development procedures, for the way designers work

and for the way they think. At the same time, we will stimulate the pupils' critical sense and their creativity (new and appropriate thinking).

- What will the pupils learn and understand?
  - Answer: The pupils will learn to observe how things function and assess their materiality, functionality and aesthetics. They will understand which things need to be considered when designing a new item or when renewing an old item. They will learn to appreciate designers' creativity and the way designers think.

- Are the tasks that we choose engaging, meaningful, practical, accessible and emotionally related to the pupils?
  - Answer: We teach pupils in sixth grade. They are used to searching for information on the internet, so they will easily find the necessary information about frames, design and designers. The task invites an emotional involvement in that picture frames are found in the children's everyday environments.

- Can the tasks and themes invite a wide cross-disciplinary involvement?
  - Answer: With this task we can bring together mathematics, physics and geometry, biology, art, woodwork and other handicrafts (design).

The teachers consider which angle they want to take and decide on what natural materials will be used.

As a warm-up to the project, the teachers and the pupils carry out a brainstorming session via dramatisation, and involving the body/senses.

The teachers run a slide show of their collection of pictures and encourage the pupils to make observations about the displayed object's functions (see the exercise: "Explanation game"). The pupils first task is an individual one: They must think it over and find a shape, a material, a function they want to study.

Explanation game

Objective: This routine promotes understanding for why something is the way it is. This routine can get children to think it over and focus on the causes or explanation of the causes.

The exercise aims to identify some interesting elements in an object or idea. "I've noticed that this object can/can be/can do/can be used for ...."

And after this remark, the teacher can ask:
"Why is it like that?"

or
"Why did it happen like that?"

(Adapted from Visible Thinking, 2009)

When they begin to draw the first version of their picture frame, the mathematics teacher supplements the work with geometric and mathematical elements and the biology teacher with some information about different types of wood. Physics can also be included if challenging shapes are chosen.

The pupils decide themselves how to go about the task by playing with the materials or by first drawing a sketch. Depending on their preferred way of thinking, the pupils choose either one of the processes. In both cases, the pupils display a great deal of diversity in problem solving.

The teachers have invited a design student as an expert for the purpose of providing the pupils with feedback in response to their work in the middle of the development process. When the student arrives, the pupils welcome him/her and give a short tour of the school when among other things, they tell the student about the rules that apply to feedback sessions at their school. In the class, the design student tells the pupils about his/her study assignments and corrects their work, using professional terms.

The pupils have the opportunity to search for the new terms and their meanings and to integrate the designer's proposals into their work.

The process is documented using photography and in the pupils' logbooks.

When the frames are finished after several feedback sessions and several versions, they are sold at the annual town festival. The revenue from the sale of the picture frames is used to finance a class trip to the Design Museum and to purchase design books for the school library.

Main theme: Make a wooden Kubb game

All of the general observations described above apply to this and the following tasks. Specifically for this project, an exercise in craftsmanship and a specific type of creativity is used: product development within fixed frameworks and an ordered task.

TASK: The aim of this learning procedure is to challenge the pupils' creativity within very fixed frameworks. The pupils will experience that the frameworks and the limitations can release a lot of creative potential. This will allow them to get first-hand experience of an artful way of thinking and creating, i.e. an experience of how professionals designers or visual artists navigate through their creative processes.

The task is about concept development, designing and producing a Kubb game, made from wood. A specific target group, for example the school's kindergarten, will have ordered the game beforehand.

WARM UP: Because the task is fixed, yet at the same time is based on creative thinking and problem solving, it is important to introduce creativity's terms and mindset. This can be either a reflection on what creativity is (see in this book: Reflection guide for creative learning processes) and/or initiating a creative exercise. A reliable exercise is the traditional "Six Thinking Hats", developed by Edward De Bono (2000) and which is based on isolating a thinking disposition and playing it against other approaches. It is recommended that the exercise that is described in the text box is dramatised and staged together with the children for the purpose of creating a playful and engaging learning environment. If the teachers choose a dramatised version they should ensure that there is enough time for an engaged a group of children who might not take a break! It is recommended that the results from this brainstorming are documented in a flip-chart and saved as a start-up for the design activity

For more details, visit: www.debonogroup.com/six_thinking_hats.php

The six thinking hats

The aim of the exercise is to supply solutions to a predetermined problem or issue by brainstorming in the following way: Each participant takes a symbolic or real hat and is obligated to develop a solution that is in concordance with its colour. The colour of the hat corresponds to an approach to a solution, such as the pessimistic, optimistic, logical, creative, etc.

The white hat: What data and information is available.

The red hat: Immediate reactions, intuitions, feelings and emotions.

The black hat: Hazards, problems, disadvantages and negative critical points.

The yellow hat: Positive and constructive solutions, optimistic approach, opportunities and advantages.

The green hat: Creative and experimental solutions, approaches that turn things on their head.

The blue hat: Organisation, strategies, definition of problems, questions, expectations, procedures, rules and frameworks.

Variation of the six thinking hats

The aim of the exercise is to supply solutions to a predetermined problem or issue by brainstorming in a way that is described in Bono's The Six Thinking Hats but with a narrative twist: Each participant "builds" his/her hat in accordance with an archetypal personality and then "wears" the symbolic or real hat and finds solutions in accordance with this archetype. Each archetype corresponds to a specific approach to problem solving.

Scrooge McDuck: What data and information is available. Focus on revenue.

Cowboy: Courage, intuition, feelings for nature and big emotions.

Voldemort: Hazards, problems, disadvantages and negative critical points. Destruction.

The Good Fairy: Positive and constructive solutions, optimistic approach, opportunities and advantages. Everything is possible and "magic".

Blockhead Hans: Creative and experimental solutions, approaches that turn things on their head. New-thinking and bold experiments.

King Arthur: Organisation, strategies, definition of problems, questions, expectations, procedures, rules and frameworks. Leadership.

DESIGN/HANDICRAFT: It is recommended that the whole process is kept going by formulating many open questions and asking the pupils to formulate open questions for their design. Because the task is fairly limited, the teacher will find it beneficial if he/she introduces a *problem finding* task together with the obvious *problem solving*.

The task can for example, be described in the following way: "To find a new version of Kubb, which will then be made out of wood". The game must meet the group's aesthetic and safety requirements. The game shall be used in a kindergarten and must be attractive and safe to play for toddlers.

Update: Engum School has continued to cultivate its interest in innovation and design and promotes projects implementing design skills.

The design activity requires some knowledge of mathematical and geometrical subjects in addition to practical woodworking skills and if required, knowledge about trees and wood as a living material. Therefore, this task invites a specifically cross-disciplinary collaboration.

EXPERT VISIT: The expert visit can be organised as a class trip rather than an external expert visiting the school. Or can include both forms: First, the expert visits the school and provides feedback about the pupils' work and with the final completion of the project, the pupils visit the expert at his/her place of work. The visit by the pupils can be usefully integrated into this project. An obvious opportunity would be to visit a toy manufacturer such as LEGO or a less well-known toy manufacturer, where the children can be given a tour and enjoy a very rewarding learning experience.

CONCLUSION: When the task is ordered, as in this case, the project will be completed when the finished work is handed over to the "customer". This can be agreed in various ways. The teacher can, for example:

- Organise an official handing over as an enjoyable social event, with participation of the entire school and school leaders
- Arrange it as a competition, where the kindergarten children choose the Kubb set they prefer and which is exhibited in a special room
- Arrange for the pupils exhibit their work in a public location.

Animation film

During the school year 2009-2010, two teachers at Nørup School in Vejle in Denmark, contacted the Animation Workshop. Based in Viborg, the Animation Workshop is the leading animation institution in Denmark. It is supported by the EU and its aim is to teach animation to school children. The teachers and Animation Workshop consultants agreed on a project where both the teachers and the pupils would learn animation techniques for the purpose of using these in teaching and learning. Specifically, they wanted to find a way to integrate animation techniques and tools into specific subjects, like Danish and

More on The Animation Workshop:
www.animwork.dk/da/en/

mathematics. The activities were practical-experiential and consisted of using animation techniques for the purpose of creating a short film, the children's feedback in response to short films that had been made elsewhere and a small "film festival" where the teachers and pupils' work was shown to parents. As a beginning, the teachers were trained in basic animation techniques and procedures by producing their own animation film and at the same time the pupils had to make a short film in two hours. The process was repeated a second time, with the teachers now acting as coaches and the Animation Workshop people functioned as expert teachers. On the second occasion, the teachers had a more systematic focus on academic subjects and the collaboration with the professional animators commenced.

STORYBOARD

A storyboard is a tool that is used in film pre-production: a drawn version of the main film scenes. Specifically, the film director and a storyboard artist and perhaps a cameraman, work together to make a storyboard for the purpose of having a visualisation of what the finished film will look like. A storyboard visualises the camera angles of each scene and gives an overview of the angles of a given space that need to be prepared and of which actors are required to be on the set.

The aim of the project was to integrate Danish, mathematics and animation and it produced many surprising results, documented in Chemi, 2010a. In the first task, the pupils in grade 2 had to learn about adjectives, verbs and nouns and the procedure was clearly introduced as a grammatical exercise. The pupils were asked to make a short film that included some people (nouns) with specific characteristics (adjectives) and an action (verb). The inspiration and the idea of the story was to come from "the 120 words", i.e. the most commonly used words in everyday speech. A stack of cards were made where each card had a single word. The pupils had to randomly pick four cards without being able to see the words. If they could not make a meaningful story with the four words they had picked, they were allowed to find their own nouns, adjectives and verbs to make a story. The pupils then had to work in groups and find a good idea for a storyboard.

The animation project provided diverse learning opportunities on many levels. The research shows (Chemi, 2010a, pp. 30-37) that there are three main learning areas that benefit from animation: Academic (academic subjects), aesthetic ability (technical and artistic tools) and mindset (artful way of thinking). When the animation is carried out in groups, social skills and teamwork skills can be added as a learning outcome. In the following section, I focus on the academic learning even though I consider that the other two areas are crucial for the individual's learning and general development.

WARM UP: When the children have to undertake a sedentary task, it can often be beneficial if they first are warmed up via a physical, sensory or aesthetic exercise. For example, singing a song, dancing to a rhythm, or playing some drums can release physical energy and the children can then navigate cognitively. If the teacher emphasises the objective of these activities, it will be easier for the children to participate and understand where they stand in the learning process.

TASKS:

1. Danish: The animated film's structure invites an almost direct translation of its elements into grammatical terms. As with Nørup School, the teachers can introduce terms like nouns, adjectives and verbs in a playful, narrative form. Other grammatical topics can be introduced: In addition to morphological word classes (e.g. place names, number words, adverbs), the class can also play with punctuation, syntax and semantics. The advantage of animation is that the very abstract grammatical terms can be visualised, simplified and dramatised, even for very young pupils.

2. Mathematics: With its time and space dimension, animation can include a number of mathematical exercises. There are many ways to do this, for example, to stage a story on film where a mathematical calculation is part of the action. For example, construct a story with different things that the children have around them and solve a mathematical task, which is to construct a story where 18 things must go through three actions or changes, so that there are only five things left at the end. In this way the mathematical task becomes a part of the way the story is told or part of the story.
   Another approach could be to use animation as part of a research field, where mathematical tasks are integrated. For example, an animation

film has a specific length, which is based on actions and pauses that vary in length. An example of a specific exercise is to measure the variability of actions and pauses using a stopwatch, which can lead to critical reflection on how long/short a pause needs to be to emphasise a specific action.

The animation's story takes place in space, which can be shown in geometric or trigonometric perspectives. If the figures are three-dimensional, three-dimensional trigonometry can be integrated. For example, the pupils choose to build 3D figures as characters in the film.

3. History/geography/religion or other humanities subjects: The animation film can represent a wide range of subjects from the humanities in a playful and artistic fashion. For example, the pupils can make a film about a historic event with a specific geography, a literary historical theme, etc.

4. Biology/physics/chemistry: The scientific subjects can also be used in animation as narrative content, in the same way that the humanities subjects can be used, or in a science theatre approach, which is described below. All of the elements and experiments in chemistry, biology and physics can be used for the purpose of creating special effects in the film. For example, effects like artificial smoke, explosions, magnetism, strange sounds, liquids, crystals, etc.

DESIGN/HANDICRAFT: The animation process consists of the following phases. A) Storyboarding, where the plot is chosen and the different shots are drawn B) Creation of the figures and the space C) Filming D) Editing and film assembly E) Adding a soundtrack. The technical tasks are quite rigid, while the creation of the figures can be based on different types of craftsmanship, such as:

1. Paper cutouts: Both the figures, props and scenes can be made from coloured cardboard cutouts.

2. Model wax: Both the figures, props and scenes can be modelled in three dimensions using model wax or clay.

3. Everyday objects: A wonderful creative exercise is to encourage the children to use things from their everyday life as their animation figures. Because these things are not created by the children, they require a "bonding" phase, for example, through an examination of the object's real or metaphorical functions.

4. Toys: A toy functions as everyday object and there is the advantage that the children have already emotionally bonded with it, therefore it will activate a playful and engaged mental approach.

5. Natural materials: These can be both three-dimensional and flat. If the teachers choose this solution, they can plan a joint trip to the countryside where the material can be found, observed, collected and studied in its natural environment. This solution invites collaboration with the biology teacher.

6. Traditional drawings: This medium often needs drawing skills, but not necessarily. A stick-man drawing would do.

EXPERT VISIT: In Denmark, major organisations like The Animation Workshop or the Danish Film Institute can provide collaboration on a voluntary basis, just as freelance animators or storyboard artists can be contacted. The procedure for the feedback sessions should follow the same procedure described in the above cases.

CONCLUSION: One way of concluding the animation activity is to arrange a general viewing for the public that includes parents, siblings, the school and people from the local community. Ideally, the staging of this should be as realistic as possible, with advertisements, admission tickets, booking of seats, sales of soft drinks and popcorn, with staff to help people find their seats and to tidy up, etc. The pupils can be involved in this set-up and academic learning can be incorporated into all of the tasks: Accounts, creating advertisement posters, project management, etc.

The animated films could also be publicised on YouTube or on a social media platform that is popular with the children.

An example of a real case

This section reports on a case that was observed in Nørup School in Vejle in Denmark (Chemi, 2010a), where the teachers integrated animation into their teaching in two different workshops as part of a single project. The project's programme covered several days and was developed in collaboration with teachers at the school and consultants from the Animation Workshop in Viborg. The teachers operated as a team every day, covering both the humanities subjects (Dorit: Danish, Christianity, music, drama) and the scientific subjects (Lone: mathematics, nature, technology, sport) and the two consultants were professional animators (Hanne and her assistant, Anker). Both the teachers and the animators had a specific interest in each other's work and approach. The teachers wanted to expand their pedagogic knowledge and practice using artist film tools and the Animation Workshop wanted to study the learning potential in animation.

Both workshops had fixed external observers. In the project's second week, in addition to myself as the researcher, there were also another two observers who also assisted: An artist with an interest in animation during the first part of the project and a newly qualified animator. During the second part of the project, other professionals who were interested in the project were also present: A consultant from the municipality and leaders and other teachers from the school.

The participating class was a second grade class, made up of 20 children (8 boys, 12 girls).

The week-long project was carried out in the class's normal classroom. There was plenty of light, with light from above and from a glass door, which led to a small internal courtyard. The classroom was colourful and spacious and very like a standard school classroom. The pupils' artworks were hung on the walls, the necessary teaching material was in a cupboard along with "extra things", such as a sofa bed, pillows, costumes, Hi-Fi system, balls, etc. The teachers had prepared the classroom beforehand and had arranged the small tables for the group work, so that they formed small workstations, each with its own camera, stand and laptop.

Each day of the second workshop started (and ended) with a class song, which the teacher would begin to sing to bring the class to order and the children would immediately sing along with the teacher. During the first day of the project week, the adults immediately noticed that the children felt secure and were curious. Shortly afterwards, Dorit and Hanne (who also had a leader function at The Animation Workshop and in this workshop) gave a recap. The pupils demonstrated that they could remember precisely in relation to the academic and technical elements, for example they easily remembered that a noun was a "thing", a verb was a movement in animation and they remembered that it was very important to have pauses and that ideally, there should not be too many pictures at once. They also remembered what the specific elements in the animation were: Figures, storyboard, background, sound, action, pauses and ideas.The week started with a specific assignment: The pupils must make a short film in no more than two hours and the film must be inspired by the "120 words". The pupils had to immediately work in groups and find a good idea for a storyboard.

The educational activities demonstrated a high level of engagement, deep concentration a good atmosphere and the practical tasks were clearly defined. The pupils appeared to be concentrating hard and really enjoying using the tools they had learned to use in the first workshop. Their animation production progressed really well and there was a complete absence of group conflicts.

The following day started with a feedback session, which focused briefly on the animations that the children had been developing.

The task for the second day was to construct a story with different things that the children had around them and to solve a mathematical task. The children got started immediately and they discussed the calculation while they focussed specifically on the storyboard.

For inspiration, they were shown an animation film featuring animated pencils that had been made by children. Afterwards, the pupils gave feedback to questions that were about understanding the actions in the film ("Do you know what it was about?", "What was it about?")

and the adults interpreted the film for them. A second animation film was shown as a conclusion to the pupils' work with the external consultants. This film had been made by a newly qualified animator who was involved in the project. This was followed up by a very short feedback session, where mainly the adults interpreted the film.

In the middle of the workshop, the teachers and observers noticed that the children had lost their enthusiasm and lacked focus on the mathematical task in the animation. It was also noticeable that the children's flow had been disrupted for a prolonged period. The teachers took note of the falling energy levels and discussed its meaning and cause during the class intervals. There had been conflicts between the pupils and this had required the teacher's attention. New groups were formed and alternative ways to find new partners were offered. After a short recap of the technical artistic animation guidelines and procedures, the day's task was introduced: Complete the film that was started the day before or begin a new film, "Freer, more voluntary." The day's programme was marked by the teacher's difficulties in integrating the academic content with the animation, and a clear diminishing of the pupils' flow and concentration, and above all the animator's hope of giving the children an experience of success. The next day the film would be shown to the parents and the whole class in a mini film festival. At first glimpse, the pupils appeared not to be concentrating and they worked in an unstructured manner, but all of the films were completed and the workshop achieved its goal with a real sense of ownership among the children and their evaluation of the workshop was positive.

Colouring book

At a school development project in Vejle in Denmark, described below as a case, the collaboration between the school and a professional painter took a specific direction in the integration of art in teaching. The project experimented with an educational design that involved the entire school and which was based on pupil collaboration across age and gender. It was planned as project activity and group learning and it was performed as a cross-disciplinary collaboration, involving the local community with contribution from an expert.

Even though this project was the result of very special circumstances, it provides learning and inspiration that can be used in other contexts. As with the other projects described in this book, all of the general observations named above apply to its organisation. Specifically for this project, there is a special link with the local community, and a particular type of creativity is used: *Community art,* within fixed frameworks and learning objectives.

TASK: To create an artwork that would decorate a particular public location with help from a professional painter and the local community.

PRELIMINARY WORK: Because this is a project where several partners collaborate, it also promotes several different ways of thinking and so it is important in the preliminary phase that the teacher looks at the special cultural encounter that the collaboration creates. Two or several cultures have to be able to talk with each other before they can work together, so it is recommended a professional coach or facilitator acts as a guide.

When it comes to the project planning, the teacher should be aware that several hours must be spent on the preliminary work.

WARM UP: As part of the preparation of the artistic activity, the teacher can arrange a trip to the nearest city. The trip can be about:

1. Looking at urban space

2. Visiting the artists' studios in the city

3. Visiting a museum or gallery with the possibility of talking with art experts

The objective of the trip can be to guide the pupils in *looking* at art, before they start *making* art. It can be beneficial if the organisation of the trip allows the pupils to learn about the artistic genre they will be involved in. For example, in the case of Andkær School in Vejle, the trip focused on public art. The teachers from Andkær School remember the day as an "eye-opener" both for the children and themselves:

> We walked about Vejle and [...] for a lot of the kids it was an eye-opener as they looked about because "if that over there is art, so the lettering in a sheet of iron must also be art because that was created by people", and so you begin to look at the old and the new and what people thought was art in the past and which now is more abstract [approach], and I actually think it was fun. (Chemi, 2010b, p. 70)

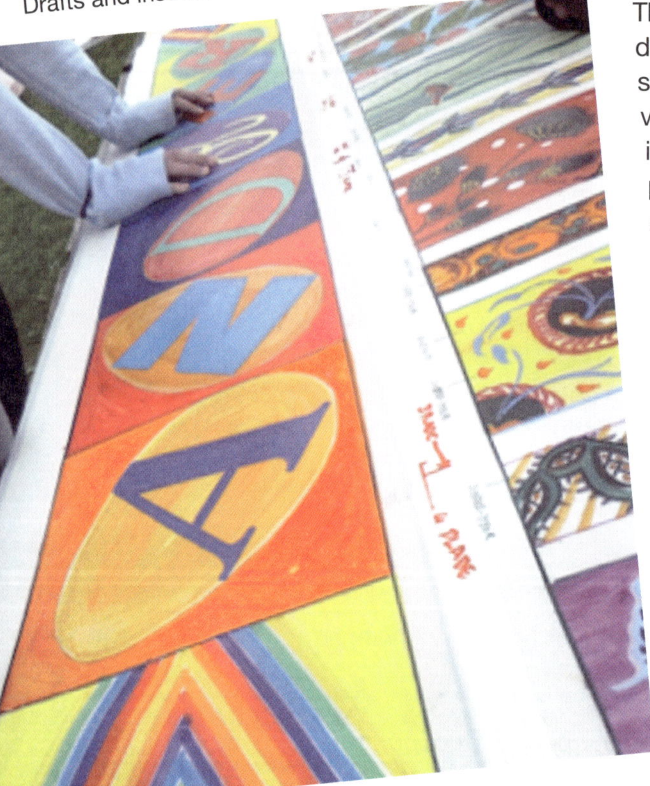

Figure 9
The artist's prototype: Drafts and instructions

The pupils can be trained to be more disposed to observing art in the urban space and be more aware of art's diversity. This trip can lead to a change in consciousness, which involves the pupils' fundamental comprehension of a tour of the city and of art. For example, *before* the study tour of the city, the pupils at Andkær School associated a trip to the city with shopping, toy shops and ice cream parlours. *Now* the children know that their nearest city offers many more fun things to look at. *Before* the trip, the children associated art with pictures hung on walls. *Now* the children know that art can take many different forms.

Even though this experience can be a revelation, it is crucial to closely guide the children in an independent observation of artworks. A deep observation of artworks is full of learning potential, which Tishman & Palmer (2007) emphasise: "Works of Art Are Good Things to Think About", but neither deep observation of, or nuanced reflection on the artworks happens by itself. The pupils must be guided closely in completing their learning. They should be helped by the teachers pointing at the artworks or details in the artworks that are worth noticing.

DESIGN/HANDICRAFT: The handicraft in this model is very simple, which makes it accessible even to very young children. It is "simply" about finding the corresponding colours from the artist's drawing and transferring them to the colouring book (see Figure 9).

The complexity of the task is not "what" the pupils shall do but "how" they shall do it. In this respect, the artist's role is to "watch over" and guide the children's quality awareness. To a great degree, the artist's role is to demonstrate in practice how an artist thinks and acts when shaping a work of art, how to talk about the material, the language and the terms that define artistic professionalism. The pupils' learning is directed towards more of an appreciation of the artist's specific language and work processes rather than any academic learning. The selected task is not very cognitively challenging in itself: The pupils will not necessarily create anything new and creative, they will not automatically express themselves, and they do not necessarily need to understand anything to carry out the task. The task might be purely mechanical and only require a low level of handicraft. This means that the children can be challenged purely in terms of aesthetic understanding and experience, which does not mean that their attention should be just focused on "the mundane work" and on the practical tasks. On the contrary, the educational design phase is tightly bound to the possibility of having a visiting artist or fixed artist connected to the project and to a relevant and cohesive feedback culture. Only in this way can the practical tasks be transformed into understanding and learning.

EXPERT VISIT: The professional artist in the artistic genre that the teachers have chosen should be present throughout. For the purpose of transferring a professional ethic, mindset and vocabulary to the pupils, the artist should be present and as attentive as possible. It would be beneficial if beforehand, the artist is informed of the school's pedagogic guidelines on how to give feedback to pupils.

During the process, the expert's role is to guide the pupils and teachers and ideally points to areas that need attention during the design process.

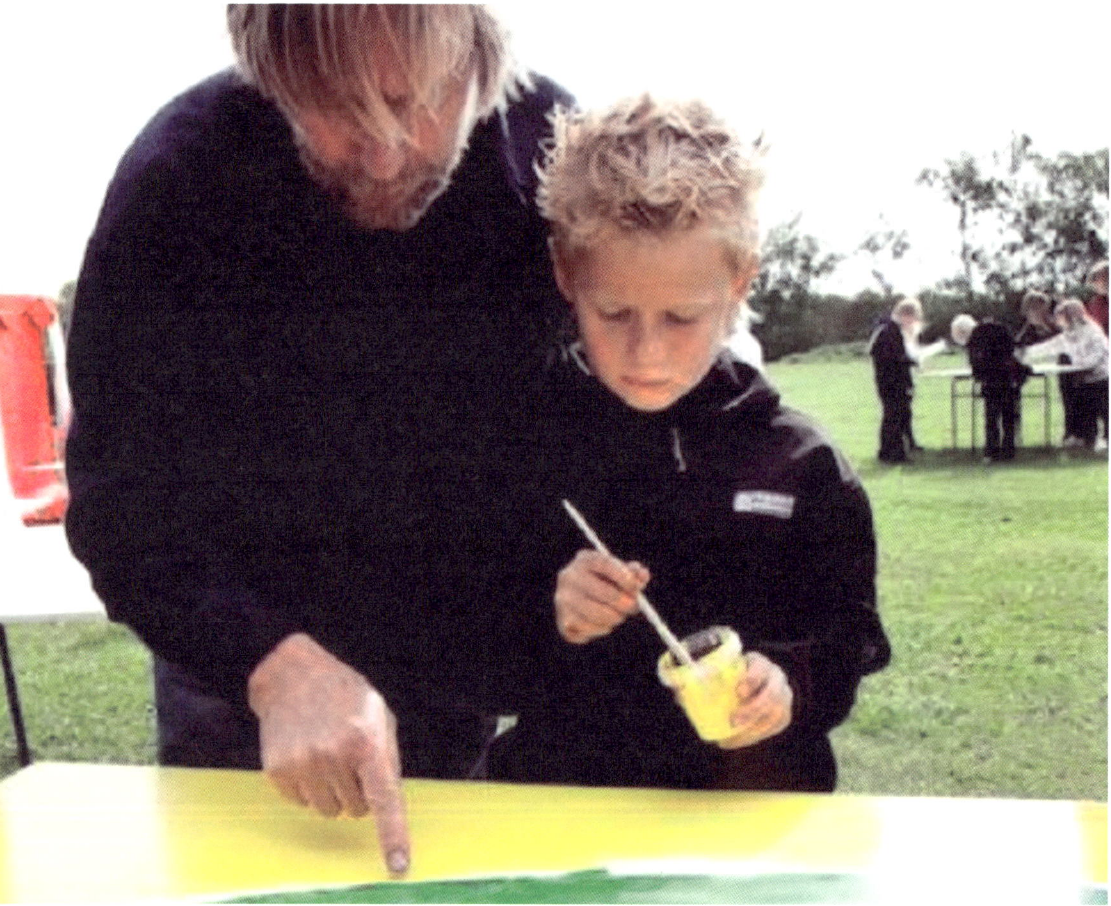

Figure 10
Artist pointing at artistic quality (photo Patrick Nielsen, 2010)

FEEDBACK SESSION: When a teaching project at the school is based on design and practical activities, the teachers are often tempted to separate the reflective and theoretical part from the practical-orientated part. In other words, if the pupils paint a picture or make a sculpture, they do not have to know anything theoretical about what they are doing and neither do they have to reflect upon their creation, just experience making the art with their senses. For perfectly good reasons, this approach was introduced into schools as a reaction to a curriculum that was exclusively theoretical. The sensory experience is often downplayed in schools, therefore teachers have a tendency to leave out reflective learning when they have an opportunity to get involved in an aesthetic project. Unfortunately, this understandable reaction prevents very good learning from artistic projects: The good experiences that the children get in these projects can lead to optimal learning, if the teacher carefully guides the process. The feedback sessions can be an extraordinary opportunity for the teachers to get the children's learning to flourish. Above all, the teachers and experts should not be afraid that it will become too difficult for the pupils. Children love to be challenged and have a need for overcoming tough challenges. Art, with its complexity and special aesthetic logic (make-believe, media, materiality, body and senses) provides an engaging learning environment. The teachers must dare to challenge the pupils with complex reflections and meta-reflections about what they have created, what they have understood and what they have appreciated.

Potential points of reflection in feedback sessions

What do you see in the artwork? (Be specific)

What works really well? Why? (Remember to point out those places where the artwork is thought to be optimal)

What does not work? Why? (Remember to be specific)

If you could change something, what would it be?

How would you change it?

What is the biggest challenge in improving the artwork?

Who could help you to do it?

Rule of thumb: If the children express a need to change the artwork they should be allowed to do so. They should always be reminded about being specific, appreciative and to look at the artwork "as artists".

Potential points of reflection in feedback sessions - continued

The pupils should be reminded to follow the following suggestions when they give feedback to each other:

Remember to be **friendly**

Remember to be **specific** (point at the specific places that require improvement)

Remember to be **helpful** (offer specific proposals for improvements)

CONCLUSION: A large development project based on the involvement of the local community and the creation of visual artworks should be celebrated both inside and outside the school. If the artworks are to be integrated into an urban space or other public location (e.g. museum, library, gallery, local hall, town hall, shopping centre), the official installation event should be covered by the press and generally get public attention. This should be taken into consideration as early as the planning phase when the teachers design the project. Naturally, the pupils should take on the main role in planning the event and on the day itself.

An example of a real case

As stated in a specific report (Chemi, 2010b), Andkær School can accurately be described as a small village school. It is located about 10 km from Vejle, has around 120 pupils and a staff of 20 (teachers, educators, leaders and technical personnel). The school has a friendly atmosphere, its location surrounded by attractive countryside. The village school building is very much typical of its type in rural Denmark, resembling a large farm building with its U-shaped structure, red brick and adjacent green areas. The school was built in 1958, extended in 1994 and again in 2004. The nearest neighbour is a kindergarten with around 30 children, who will eventually become pupils at the school. The children progress from the kindergarten through to sixth grade, after which they study at a secondary school called Gauerslund School.

Despite its apparent ordinariness, Andkær School has a very positive view of its attractive physical surroundings, which is documented in the school's responses to the physical settings questions in the first survey in MMALP (Knoop et al., 2009). Responding to the survey, 77 % of the school staff were proud or *very* proud of the school's **outdoor areas** (54 % *very* proud and 23 % proud); 61 % were proud or *very* proud of the school's **indoor areas** (however, in comparison to the outdoor areas, 15 % were *very* proud and 46 % were proud); and 39 % were proud or very proud of the school's **classrooms** (proud 8 %, *very* proud 31 %).

Physical settings								
	Agree			Neutral			Disa-gree	Don't know*
I am proud when I show the school's outdoor areas to colleagues when they visit	54%	23%	8%	15%	0%	0%	0%	0%
I am proud when I show the school's indoor areas to colleagues when they visit	15%	46%	23%	8%	0%	8%	0%	0%
I am proud when I show the school's classrooms to colleagues when they visit	8%	31%	38%	15%	0%	0%	8%	0%

Figure 11 Excerpt from MMALP, first survey

The school's project idea was based on "expanding the positive attitude linked to the physical settings" through a unique collaboration with a professional and well-known painter. The idea was to improve the underpasses and the public road that lead to the school using artworks created through a collaboration between the artist and the pupils at the school. The pupils at the school would paint pictures with help from a professional artist and hang their paintings in the public space. At the same time, the local community would support the project and provide resources, financing and a public space for the works. Furthermore, the public space would be the actual route that the children took to school, i.e. when the project was to be completed, their paintings would remind them of the project for a long time to come.

The formalised collaboration between the local culture association and the school would support the coming painting project in the form of, for example a support group, which would be responsible for the financial and organisational challenges. As is often the case in small local communities, there was a spin-off thanks to the fact that the chairman of the parents association and the chairman of the culture association was the same person. This meant that the decision-making process and communication was easier and more effective.

In only a few weeks, the project was ready with a clear design and a more detailed description, and an agreement was reached between the parties to create the pictures during a week in spring. Before this, the appointed coordination group from the school (a teacher leader and two teachers) met with the artist, the school's leadership, parent representatives and the local recreational association.

A professional painter, well-known from a TV programme[1] was headhunted via the school board's network who would guide the coordination group in planning the project week, and in kick-starting the project week and in helping complete the artworks. The school leader reported that the objective of the project was first and foremost to create a link between a space for reflection or learning and reflection in practice. Through a reflective process, it might be possible to see this movement from practice to reflection and vice versa. The leadership's main ambition was:

- To show that teaching could be done in different ways.

1 See for example, the lifestyle programme "Room Service", http://sputnik-dyn.tv2.dk/series/roomservice.

- That at the same time, the school's common goal could be achieved ("which the teachers were a bit nervous about").
- That art is something that you can help create by expressing yourself.
- That art is not just what you see on television.
- To give those pupils who struggle in ordinary classes an extra chance, so that they can be assessed on different levels and with different parameters.
- To show the world what the school can do.

The school staff described the project as "a way of giving the school a profile". The school had already initiated a systematic branding strategy in the form of a "Branding Group" with think-tank functions that discussed the following: How will Andkær School survive in the future? In addition to a collaboration, Erik Peitersen's involvement meant press coverage and exposure for Andkær School[2].

The coordination group's expectations for the project were:

- The children would personally create the final artwork, so that it would be what they wanted to express and not what the artist wanted to create.
- Strengthened social skills: The children would collaborate, use each other's resources "in another way" and do work that was based on their own strengths.
- The pupils would experience pride in their work and their school.

The coordination group's expectations of the teacher's role was very clear. The teachers would:

- Challenge the children to try again and spend time on the artwork.
- Challenge the pupils' critical sense by teaching them to "look at things".
- Make proposals.
- Teach the pupils not just to look at things, but rather to look at things in a different way.

---

2 See for example, broadcast from TV Syd, 31 May 2010 (scroll to 13:00) www.tvsyd.dk/arkiv/2010/05/31/?video_id=29936. Or local newspaper "Vejle Amts Folkeblad" (Bang, 2010).

The painting project was strengthened by different coordination meetings, which were held in preparation. All of the involved parties discussed the development of the project at these meetings, ideas and solutions were deliberated in collaboration and the project was planned. The artist's role was defined by an artistic mindset. Peitersen's contribution to the planning phase was of a practical, artistic nature and often took its point of departure on what could actually be achieved in practice. With his extensive expertise and experience in working with artistic materials and techniques, Peitersen guided the coordination group's ambitions towards a project that was technically feasible and artistically appealing. The challenge was in merging both the pedagogic elements (which the coordination group conveyed) and the legal requirements (which the board was in control of) with a full artistic experience.

In the model shown in Figure 12, the artist's role in the preparation phase was to turn the (now and then intense) debate between the board and the coordination group, into a practical solution. An important aspect of the preparation meeting was that Peitersen often reminded the other participants about how long it takes to create an artwork. Running the risk of being a "killjoy", time and time again, he had to respond to the educators' many good and often exciting ideas with: "But it takes time ..." Based on his responses to the educators' ideas, it is clear how Peitersen relates to the artistic planning: The colours must dry, the panels must be cut, the colour quality must be durable, proportions and drawings must match, etc. He gives feedback to proposals for materials: Acrylic might be fun for a shelter but is horrible to work with and it cracks in icy conditions, ceramics take too long to make and do not last.

The educators and the artist's cultures often clashed, for example, when decisions had to be made about the basic choices: Should it be the artist or the children who produce the artwork? On the one hand, the artist would guarantee the quality of the work in relation to the authorities by submitting a drawing and signing the official application. On the other hand, the educators maintained the artwork should be "the children's expression". The coordination group envisioned

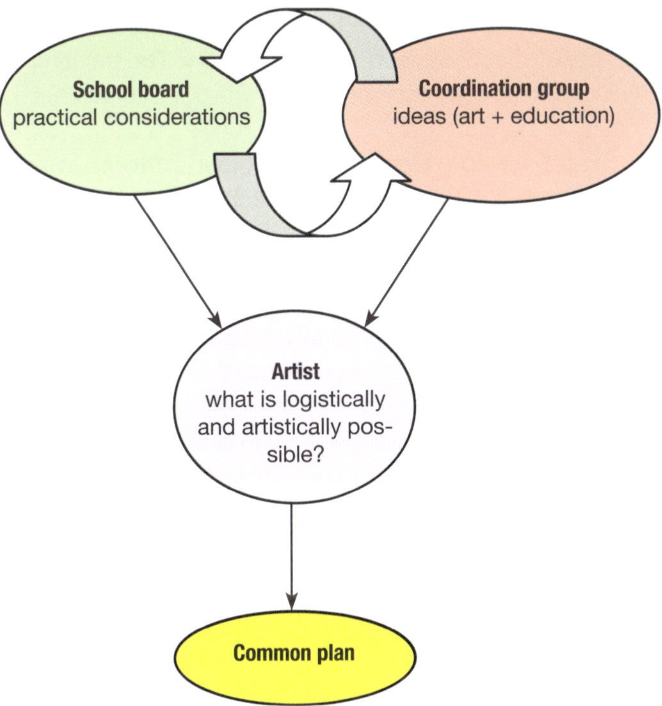

Figure 12 Collaboration model

strengthening the art from the child's perspective, where the collaboration with a professional artist would ensure the finished product would be "more complete": "It's about getting things completed properly". Peitersen's agreement to prepare a drawing based on the school's input, ideas and wishes was a provocation as far as the educators were concerned, and caused some dissatisfaction - a completely controlled process was not what they had imagined. Where was the children's self-expression? What opportunity did the pupils have to develop their creativity? Where did ownership lie?

Despite these reservations, the coordination group organised the project week in accordance with the colouring book model. It ended in success despite the reservations.

Peitersen's drawing was finally approved and appeared to match the educator's wishes: The same colours and patterns were repeated for the purpose of cohesion and recognisability. The painting project became in effect a huge colouring book, which Peitersen had created on the basis of the educators' ideas and made on large wooden panels. The concept was to create two large colourful friezes, which would be installed in the local underpass on each side. Each frieze was made distinctive through the use of a specific visual pattern, one made up of geometric figures and letters (the school's name) and the other was based on the natural world (flowers, fish, leaves). These friezes would be as long as the underpass, so several panels were made, each panel was 2.44 x 1.22 m and these were used to create a colouring book. The educators were immediately disappointed because the children's task was to just colour in areas on the panels. But in fact Peitersen's colouring book ended up being a very positive challenge for both the pupils and the teachers.

The project was executed in the school's spacious playground, which had a camp fire area, climbing frames, sandbox, a wide lawn and "Musse", an old fishing boat that the children could play on.

On the very first day, the children were given a short introduction, which aimed to establish a clear framework for the whole week and get the work started. The personnel from the school focussed on the overall concepts behind the project while the artist introduced the practical aspects by describing the project as "fixed" and "drawn already" because of the public approval and at the same time emphasised the unique contribution that the children could make ("your unique brush stroke"). In addition, Erik Peitersen explained the thinking behind the drawings that he had developed: "I've thought about that instead of painting lots of ducks [Andkær School > Danish "and" = duck], it should be something round [Andkær School > Danish "kær" = pond, a little almost round body of water] and resemble what we call in art, a *frieze*" (Chemi, 2010b, p. 29).

From an artistic perspective, Peitersen's choice of frieze as a visual expression is in harmony with the nature of the main task (making the sides of an underpass that leads to the school more decorative) and the co-ordination group's wish for the paintings' theme to be related to nature. Friezes are used in architecture as decorative elements on building structures such as facades or columns and often use nature as an iconographic theme. In general, friezes are often a series of regular panels that alternately repeat geometric themes and themes inspired by nature (see the reproduction of the friezes of *The Circus* in Bath, UK, in Figure 13).

To support the process, Peitersen prepared and brought the following material:

FRIEZE

Frieze (Italian fregio, Latin Phrygius) was in ancient architecture the decorative part of the main cornice, found just below the building's roof. In general, a frieze is defined as an ornamental relief.

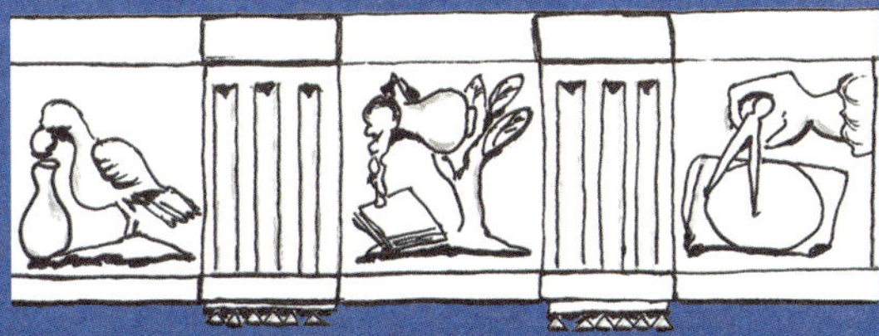

Figure 13
Reproduction of the frieze at The Circus in Bath, UK

- Scaled down drawings on paper of the finished work with numbered colour fields.
- Large white wooden panels, prepared with drawings that corresponded with the scaled down drawings on paper.
- Extra white wooden panels.

The task was to find the correct colour and paint the large white panels, exactly as they were represented on the paper drawing. The correspondence between the drawings and the panels was easy to understand, so that the children could find their way around the panels on their own or with some help from the older pupils, teachers or a family member who was present during the week.

There were short instructions on the drawings and the colours were numbered. The pupils went to work immediately and much to the teachers' surprise and satisfaction, were very effective. They quickly found their way to the painting station and split up into groups. Then the work began. At first glance the process appeared chaotic, creative and there was a pleasing atmosphere, balanced by a stringent structure that supported the project all week.

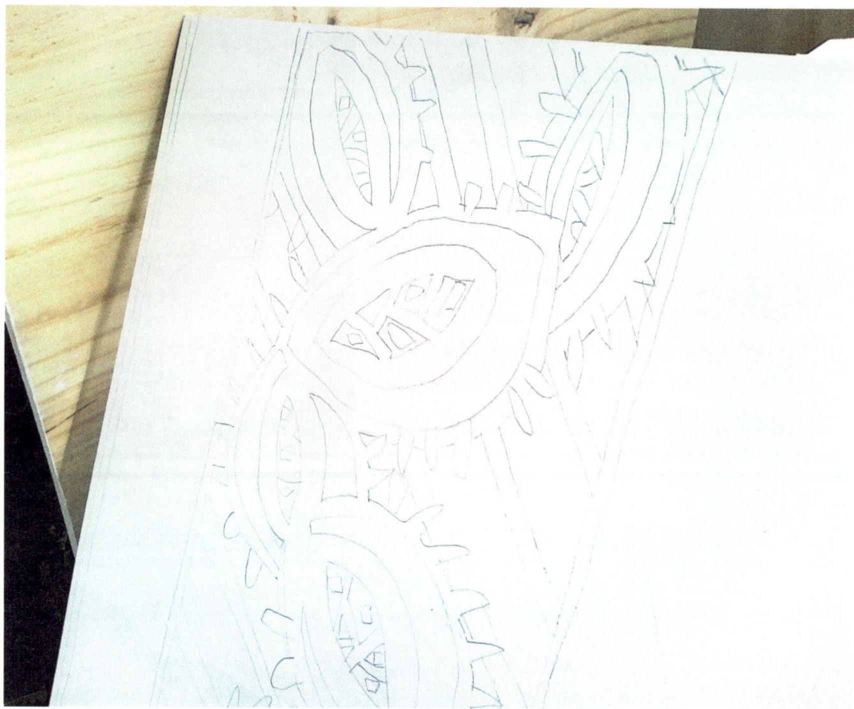

Figure 14
Peitersen's colouring book

The working groups were formed on the basis of where the pupils lived in relation to the locations where the finished artwork was to be installed. In consideration of the children who would not be involved in the painting, the coordination group created a media group with an assigned teacher and this group documented the whole project. The media group set up a permanent media station in the school library where the group could use computers and other technical equipment. Here the group could disseminate interesting documentation of the painting process near to the library's glass doors.

The coordination group included different structured games in the activity plan (for example, rounders, a spitting competition and other games coordinated by the "play patrol") and free play, so that the pupils could decide when they needed to take a break and what to do during the break. The structured games and some of the unstructured games were based on the older children's active involvement: The older children watched over the younger ones, especially when curiosity was too much for some of the smaller children and they overstepped the activity boundaries. The older pupils ensured there was a safe transition, both physically by holding the younger ones by the hand and by ensuring they didn't hit each other and mentally, by explaining what was going on or by answering the younger pupils' questions.

The teachers, along with Peitersen as the expert, supported the process on an on-going fashion. The feedback sessions were not detailed or critical but achieved the goal of communicating the mindset of an artist to the pupils.

When the paintings were finished, they were shown to parents at a preview exhibition in the school and thereafter they were installed in the public site as had been planned.

Play/games

Play and games can be very engaging ways of stimulating learning and can work relatively very easily and they are simple to integrate into teaching. The playful learning processes are based on the individual's desire and need to learn and develop through play (Huizinga, 1955). These processes, like the artistic processes, can be sensory and aesthetic. However, research shows that the pupils can come to doubt their own learning if the connection between playing and learning is not made explicit, especially from the start (Chemi, 2011). Remember the pupils at B School who asked: "What has today got to do with mathematics?" (Unpublished interview, Vejle Municipality, 2010), even though the teachers' intention was to teach mathematics through play and even though they had invested a lot of hours, energy and resources in designing fun learning activities for the whole school.

WARM UP: A task that integrates play and games with learning should be started by telling the pupils what the teachers' objective are. The teachers should spend some time on preparing the pupils on a learning exercise via play and games. It should be made explicit which subjects and topics are in focus ("You will learn some mathematics and logical thinking via computer and a board game"). The practical part of the teachers' preparation should involve a hunt for intelligent play and games that the pupils can be involved in.

TASK: For example, Sudoku, which can be used to learn to think mathematically, a quiz about different subjects, a computer game for different historical narratives (Sims; World of Warcraft), etc. Because many of contemporary educational materials already use a play approach (crossword puzzle, rhymes and lists of words, geometric puzzles, etc.), teachers can consider arranging a special event, where outdoor play that requires physical activity can be the largest part of the learning experience. The pupils often look for changes to their everyday routines and old games in a new setting can re-kindle their interest. This *arousal* should make them more receptive to learning but the connection between the experience and the conscious learning should always be emphasised and guided by the teachers. The great advantage of integrating play and games in teaching is the amount of playing, games, board games, computer games that are available, which are free or inexpensive.

DESIGN/HANDICRAFT: Play and games often lack the design dimension found in artistic activities. However, it is possible to include design tasks in play, for example in a game where the player has to guess a drawing or LEGO sculptures, or where the game consists in building virtual realities as in Minecraft.

EXPERT VISIT: Because play and games are connected with leisure and hobbies, it will be difficult to find professional experts in this field, unless teachers are willing to contact professional players or "gamers" (video games, chess players) or toy manufacturers. The experts in this field are the children themselves. There are no others better than they are when it comes to playing together and to playing games. Therefore, the teacher may consider involving this expertise. It will invite a dialogue between pupils, where the older pupils who are more experienced in play and games, can guide the younger pupils. This ensures both ownership and *peer education* (Damon, 1984, and Webb, 2010). Last but not least, the children's mutual learning and teaching, which is a natural part of their world, is incorporated into the school. In the published literature, situations where children teach each other are defined as informal learning environments. By making space for these learning relationships and by including them in the school's formal teaching, the school will be able to utilise a large degree of the engagement that is created and experienced in informal learning settings.

CONCLUSION: In contrast to the artistic experience, play is often competitive. Therefore, a natural conclusion would be to name the best competitor (individual or group). For the purpose of a positive competitive spirit, the teacher may consider developing a concluding event that is both fun and entertaining for all.

Drama: Science theatre

Science theatre is a very popular hybrid in theatre that presents scientific subjects to audiences. It is based on the theatre's propensity for educational forms of communication and content. In one form or another, theatre has always utilised educational elements or ideals. In other words, throughout its development, theatre's objective has been, among others, to teach, inform, convince and instruct. For example, ancient Greek theatre had a clear educational role in sharing its ideals, cultural visions, values and knowledge in dramatic form and a socio-political role in supporting the community. In the modern interpretation of science theatre, it is evident there is a trend for reliving the original relationship between science and performance, which was lost in Western culture during the Enlightenment.

Science theatre has shown itself to be a creative, sensory and experience-rich way of presenting difficult scientific concepts and subjects. An additional benefit with this form of teaching and performing is that it has different functions and dramaturgical typologies, which can be used for different purposes and in different contexts. For example, the following typologies (read more in Chemi & Kastberg, in press) show what is special for specific forms of theatre, which type of presentation or communication it creates and which type of learning can it be compared to:

- Transmission

Transmission is about sending messages out with as little interruption as possible. The classic delivery of a monologue speech is an example of this traditional form of theatre performance, where the actors stand on the stage while the audience sits below in the stalls and listens in silence. Transmission examples are the plays: Brecht's *Galileo*, about the Italian scientist or the Danish *Den Magiske Kugle (The Magic Bullet*), a work where students and researchers demonstrated through drama how scientific ideas arise and develop.

- Interaction

This form of drama is about establishing an action-reaction dynamic, such as demonstrations or "shows", where science students carry out experiments in front of pupils in schools and in upper secondary schools. The interaction takes place during the experiments. In Denmark, *Fysikshow (Physics Show), Kemishow* (Chemistry Show) or *Natur-i-teltet* (Nature in the Tent) are popular examples where selected physics experiments (e.g. magnetism, low pressure) or chemical experiments (e.g. combustion, smoke, explosions) are carried out. The form of learning is dialogic, experience-based and experimental.

- Transaction

This form is based on establishing a close connection between the sender and receiver, where together they construct a message and a mutual understanding. The most distinctive example of this form of theatre in Denmark is Mathematics Theatre, which has been developed by Klaus Rubin, Peter Müller and Marikka Andreasen for Ellekær School in Aarhus. At Ellekær School, the pupils do not just receive communication (transmission paradigm), neither are they chosen to only react to the inputs which now must come from an expert (interaction paradigm); in this case the children are co-producers of the knowledge. Both children and teachers take on roles, there are number thieves and pirates at play, a volcano becomes a truncated cone, learning by rote becomes spoken lines and everything takes place in a great performance about mathematics. The form of learning for this purpose is project and collaboration based.

Fantasy exercises

Always say "Yes."
- "Hi. Are you the one who stole my ice cream?"
- "Yes."
- "I'm going to call the police right now."
- "Yes. Agreed."
- "Are you crazy or what?"
- "Yes. I have just been released from the asylum."

Always say "No."
- "Do you love me?"
- "No."
- "Shall we get divorced?"
- "No. Let's not."

And so on ...

WARM UP: Any actor training techniques can be used for the purpose of warming up for a presentation or exercise in science theatre (Johnstone, 1996; Spolin, 2000; Zinder, 2002). Teachers should be aware that both the imagination and body should be prepared for a creative dramatisation. Therefore, the teacher may choose warm-up exercises that both stimulate the individual's body and their ability to imagine.

Physical exercises

The body can think just as effectively as the brain and more creatively. To move around freely in a room leads to physical observations that the brain may not notice. To warm-up in this dimension pupils can:

Mirror each other

Mirror each other with associations and variations

Move around the room as if they are: three metres high, are dwarfs, paralysed in one leg, are babies, a hairdresser, a fashion model, a farmer, etc.

Throw a ball at each other and at the same time shout out an imaginary name.

TASK: The artistic form can be used to communicate scientific and academic subjects or to stage topics and concepts. Some examples are given below:

1. History and other humanities subjects can be dramatised by using two opposite positions for a specific subject. This exercise will stimulate the pupils into understanding different perspectives and to critically examine different points of view.

Historical court cases

The pupils are split into two groups and prepare arguments for and against a specific subject. The class selects two representatives, one from each group, who shall oppose one another in a court case. Other pupils improvise in the role as judge, lawyer, etc. The remaining pupils in either group support their respective representative. Examples of critical historical debates:

Does the earth orbit the sun? (Galileo versus Copernicus)
Should Jewish people be treated as criminals? (Hitler versus Einstein)
Should violence be opposed? (Gandhi versus Che Guevara)

2. Biology, chemistry and physics can be used as subjects as either dramaturgical elements by dramatising concepts from biology or physics or events, such as photosynthesis, the lifecycle of the salmon, chromosomes, the voyage of Darwin, etc., or used as a dramaturgic tool that can create fascination, such as the shows and demonstrations performed in the Kemishow (Chemistry Show), Fysikshow (Physics Show), Natur i Teltet (Nature in the Tent), where chemistry, physics and biology students perform scientific experiments using comedy and surprise as part of the show. A third way of using these subjects in a dramaturgic form is by involving knowledge from chemistry, biology and physics on stage as background knowledge for special effects or dramaturgical solutions. For example, the need to know about the force of gravity when hanging from a roof

and hoping the rope will hold, the need to know about chemical reactions to create an explosion or other special effects.

3. Mathematics. Who would have thought that numbers could dance, sing and be played? This is exactly what, Mathematics Theatre does with great success: it playfully stages calculations for and with children.

DRAMATISATION/HANDICRAFT: Theatre handicraft consists of several media and sensory impressions. Both audiences and directors require different competencies: Figurative, musical, spatial, relational, narrative, dramatic, physical, and often these days, film and digital competencies. All of these media contribute to the most complex art form people use for artistic expression. Theatre's complexity is what makes it unique and what makes it challenging. A pedagogic theatrical project should explore theatre's many different levels and forms and guide the pupils in being able to read dramatic texts. Crucial to this process is an ongoing feedback session, which unites the practical tasks with reflection and mutual criticism. If the actors do not have the opportunity to meta-reflect over their actions and movements, then they cannot learn from an art form that is very "transient". Theatre's artworks, unlike visual art for example, are not fixed and can only be captured by the audience's and actors' memory. The digital media can help by partially documenting a performance but it cannot reproduce the most important elements: The actors' physical presence and the actions' spontaneity.

Nevertheless, it is possible to evaluate a performance by giving an account of the theatre event and by using recollection. Even if the teacher is not an expert in drama or drama pedagogy or there is no possibility of collaborating with a drama teacher, he or she can still work with science theatre. Even though in this book I advocate that experts (artists) should be involved in the school projects, teachers should not solely depend on artists and the resources needed to involve them at the exclusion of everything else. If the teachers want to start creative activities in school, then that is what they should do.

The expertise can be found in professional artistic environments and achieved via an artful integration of culture, which Nørup School and Andkær School succeeded in doing.

If the teacher is interested in theatre but not an expert in drama, the following checklist can help as a way of maintaining focus on the elements that are specific for any theatrical performance.

- Space: Theatre is action that takes place in a space. The actors must be able to affect the space and create a magical aura around themselves, which the audience recognises as "performance".
- Time: Another crucial element is time, because a theatre performance happens in real time, during a specific period of time that unites the actors and the audience. This time can be a long shared experience or a very quick action or event (happening). Time in the form of rhythm adds a specific quality to the performance and therefore the actors should always be aware of pauses and speed of movements or lines.
- Movement in the space: The dramatic actions are always physical, sometimes they are just body movements or positions, other times they consist of movements in the space. All of the actors should be aware of this dimension and instructed in how to move in the space in the best possible fashion for the role or the play.
- Body and voice: They are the most important tools an actor has for communicating with the audience. Everything about an actor's physical postures and voice is meaningful and creates meaning. Many creative solutions can be examined via these tools or challenged by these tools, which can be done by experimenting with the exercise described in the text box *Obstruction*.

Obstruction

The Danish choreographer Palle Granhøj, has developed a technique for stimulating the dancers' and actors' creativity in their physical expression. He asks a dancer to find an action and to keep repeating this action in the room

Obstruction - continued

until the dancer is touched on a given area of the body, which is the signal that means the dancer must not repeat the action with that particular part of his or her body. For example, if a dancer mimes/dances an action of hitting a nail into something, he or she must continue until the dancer is touched on the neck. From that point on, the dancer must find a way of miming/dancing the action of hitting a nail into something without moving his/her neck. The exercise can continue, for example with the arm or the hand now being touched, which now makes any kind of hammering a nail action very challenging (see also Chemi, Jensen & Hersted, in press).

- Scenography, props and costumes are used to emphasise the performances atmosphere and to create even more meaning. Everything is meaningful on the stage, so if an actor walks onto the stage with an umbrella, it is because it is a necessary for the action or atmosphere.
- Lighting and sound can be very simply designed but need to be taken into consideration for every performance. Considerations must cover the most basic of requirements (Can the audience hear the lines? Can the audience see the actors?) and the more expressive requirements (does the lighting and sound effects reflect the atmosphere of the play?).
- Dramaturgy is the structure of the performances' narrative.
- Text/lines are not always necessary. If an improvisational dramatic form is chosen, the lines will be unpredictable and often have a musical flow.
- The feedback sessions in theatre are often coordinated by the director, whose role is to inspire all of the players and to get them (literally and metaphorically) to act together.
- Auditions, previews, premieres are a necessary progression towards a dramatic artwork.

EXPERT VISIT: A continuous collaboration with a theatre expert (actor, director, dramaturgist) will be optimal, rather than a limited expert visit. It is recommended that the teacher contacts a theatre group or freelance actor or an established theatre school or college and explores options for collaboration.

CONCLUSION: A public performance is a natural conclusion to the science theatre project. It can be designed as a genuine theatrical performance with ticket sales and purchase, advertising, sales in the foyer, preparation of brochures and/or a filmed version that can be viewed online. In both cases, the pupils should be involved and be active in all stages of the process.

An example of a real case

The Danish regional project called Project Zero (www.projectzero.dk) had the objective for the Danish town of Sønderborg and surrounding area to be carbon neutral by 2030. To achieve this objective, a project group started several activities, including accessible communication for families with young children. The first challenge for Project Zero was to reach out to children and teenagers: How could they present environmental issues in an engaging, fun and different form of media? How could ecology talk to the youngest children, who represent our sustainable future? The encounter with theatre-maker Ditte Aarup was a revelation for Project Zero because she was able to translate environmental issues into a theatrical, physical, emotional and seductive language. Ditte Aarup writes books and stages performances for young children. She is a specialist in writing, drawing, painting and singing about princesses, treasure and funny animals, and expert in staging original modern fairy tales for children and families (www.eventyrvaerksted.dk). The choice of the fairy tale as a genre was an obvious one, considering the project involved a very young target group. The young audience appeared to understand the subject and seemed enthralled and engaged with the art form.

Aarup performed her puppet-and-actor fairy tale by means of a low-technology portable stage. The show began in a classic way: lights were dimmed, the music began to play and the actress began to speak. She was in the role of a very modern lamp with shiny silver gloves and a charming gait. She told the story of three unlucky household appliances: light bulb Elly, radiator Randi and tap Vandfred, whose owners had never switched them off. Elly was the new one in the house and thought that the chance to be on all of the time was a very pleasing one, despite her new friends telling her to be moderate. Unfortunately, after a while she began to feel tired and her first positive feelings turned to dreadful unease.

The storyteller interacted with the audience and told them to try and find a solution to Elly's exhaustion. She even sang to emphasise a couple of conceptual turning points and this involved the young audience in the hunt for a solution to Elly's problem. The youngest children who sat on the floor or chairs in traditional rows were encouraged and instructed to dance and sing. They summoned a magician, who conjured up a decisive solution: He was able to switch off Elly, who then regained power and became calm.

This very simple plot is the dramaturgical background for the Danish children's theatre's performance *Eventyret om elpæren og vandhanen* (The Adventure of the Light Bulb and the Tap), written by and featuring Ditte Aarup Johnsen. The puppet theatre play was written for children aged 3-7 years, as part of Project Zero in Southern Denmark. Because the puppet play focuses on energy and energy consumption, and aims at introducing children and their families to environmental issues it can be categorised as Science theatre (Chemi & Kastberg, in press).

Expeditionary Learning: hydrogeology

A journey of discovery in the Expeditionary Learning tradition is a learning journey that starts with the pupils' curiosity and interest. This form of learning does not mean that the children only get involved in things that they were already interested in. Rather, the teachers excite and stimulate the pupils' interest with specific tools and educational forms. The following is an account of a concrete learning expedition project, which is partly described in Berger (2003) and partly personally reported by the author in an interview I conducted with him in 2008 (Cambridge, MA, USA).

More about Expeditionary Learning

The schools' website: http://elschools.org/

Film with pupils at conference: http://vimeo.com/21971534

This particular learning expedition started with a teacher (Ron Berger), who was contacted by a close friend, who also happened to be a Professor in Geology. This friend was well-informed about Berger's teaching methods. Berger's friend had just acquired a machine that could analyse water quality and wanted to loan it to the school so that it could be used for teaching purposes. After some consideration, Berger decided to apply for a grant to finance a project. At the same time, he started to meet with geologists, experts in measuring water and read the literature that they referred him to. He networked and discovered a former student had a relative who could advise him on GIS mapping and cartography.

The school received funding and the experts in the teachers' network became attached to the project on a voluntary basis.

To prepare the pupils for making comprehensive hydrogeological measurements that have never been made before in their geographical area, Berger decided to challenge the pupils with a less complex task: To measure pollution in the river's surface water by using an inexpensive chemistry kit designed for use by children in secondary school. The tasks consisted of collecting the data in the field and analysing different things: pH level, nitrates, oxygen, etc.

The pupils were in grade 4 and they were considered by many to have behavioural problems and not able to pass the national standardised tests. However, they were quite able to manage the chemistry kits and take the water samples with care and professionalism.

A couple of university students enthusiastically joined the project and analysed the data. The report was written and concluded, with contributions from all of the pupils and then presented to the authorities with a great deal of pride: "A student with profound reading and writing learning disabilities was one of the strongest in the class in computer-based analysis. A student with a serious medical syndrome that made much school-work impossible had been very competent in the field, completing water tests with real understanding" (Berger, 2003, p. 112).

After this preparation phase, the pupils were ready to carry out the main task: To study all of the private wells in the town. The teaching was organised across different subjects (science, mathematics, English, technology, social studies), and art supported the entire process, especially in the written presentation (layout, writing, visual communication, design and preparation of graphs and tables). In addition, the whole project had an artful approach: The explorer organised the teaching so that it resembled an artist process with its cycles, quality awareness, attention to materiality, feedback sessions with focus on action-oriented changes (within Expeditionary Learning, feedback sessions are known as "critique sessions", which corresponds to the language of the art studio), etc.

The pupils worked hard and were motivated for many days in a row. "Did they take this work seriously? You bet they did. People's health depended on their accuracy. The whole town, and lots of nervous families, were anxiously awaiting their findings. When we got our first data sheets with test results, each child in class analyzed the results of a particular family well in order to prepare a report for the family. We were about fifteen minutes into the study analyses when one boy noticed a level of a metallic element that was above federal standards. He began to cry. Other students gathered around him. Though we had discussed this for weeks and had memorized federal standards exactly for this purpose, it took on a new meaning when it was real data. This was a family's drinking water; this affected the life of a Kindergartner in our school, a boy we knew and loved" (Berger, 2003, pp. 112-113).

When the children are given meaningful, challenging, manageable and "real" tasks, the teacher's only problem is not how to motivate the children but how to drag them away from the work so they can take a break!

This learning expedition concluded with a final task: a letter was written for each family. This letter presented the individual results for each well and explained what the results meant. The letters also contained background information about critical findings and proposals for how the issue could be tackled. To finish, the class collected all of the results in a summary report, written in accordance with rigorous scientific standards, with hypotheses, research questions, data results and recommendations, which was finally made available online in a custom-made website and submitted to local politicians.

Any teachers who want to organise teaching as expeditionary learning, should know that Ron Berger's project lasted several months. There was no quick access to learning, rather the learning process was slow. A detour, which resulted in surprising success stories and robustness: "The mother of one of the students who worked on the project, looked at me and said: My son will never be the same. No matter how many tests tell him he's stupid, he knows he's not. He did that work. He knows he's capable of excellence" (Berger, 2003, p. 116).

Mindfulness

I believe that a mindful approach is a large part of an artistic experience and of the creative process. Presence, full contact with your body, mind and your relationships with the world around you, feeds the artistic life stories and narratives. This is the background to my own term Artfulness, which brings together the inward-looking insight from mindfulness and the external expression from art.

Despite the huge self-development potential that is inherent in mindfulness, it is still not widely accepted or used in schools. There is only a limited amount of published academic literature related to mindfulness in Denmark, but there is some qualified proposals about the possibility of integrating mindfulness in learning and pedagogy (see Rotne & Rotne, 2011). This chapter will provide some inspiration for integrating mindfulness in the school.

Mindfulness is a meditative tool for attaining a deep state of concentration, which results in a regulation of the body, mind and relationships.

Regulation of:
- Body (regulation of stress)

- Mind (awareness training)
- Relationships (stimulation of empathy and compassion)

In Buddhism, mindfulness ensures the individual's journey towards wisdom and deep insight through specific meditative practice, aimed at finding inner peace and being at peace with one's self. Western psychologists, therapists and organisational theorists have used the term in their professional areas of expertise, benefiting from a holistic approach to people.

Mindfulness is also used in therapy and clinical interventions, for example Jon Kabat-Zinn has systematically utilised mindfulness to minimise pain, anxiety and stress, as a way of activating a **coping** strategy in the case of illness (Kabat-Zinn, 1990; Kabat-Zinn, 1994) or in teaching and learning.

An example of the specific contribution that mindfulness makes in pedagogy would be the concept's positive impact in learning and transfer situations (see Salomon & Globerson, 1987) or in the creation of positive emotions, which strengthen a flexible anti-authoritarian pedagogical culture, which is aware of different perspectives (Langer, 1993). The obvious outcome of mindfulness in pedagogy is the strengthening of awareness: If it is correct, as flow theories claim, that the potential competencies or intelligences cannot be developed optimally if the individual cannot learn to control and guide his or her attention (Csikszentmihalyi, 2000; Csikszentmihalyi, 1990), then mindfulness can be a way of moving towards support of a flow structure, where stillness, flexibility and creativity are cultivated. Especially the non-judgemental positive attitude can be a way of supporting the children's tolerance, self-confidence and self-worth. The biggest challenge in using mindfulness in the schools is perhaps in the case of difficult children or children who are not resilient, who often act on urges, even before they have learned to notice them. This is a very interesting potential application of mindfulness because it can help to create resilient children but more empirical data need to be collected about this.

Mindfulness training can lead to an acceptance of that everything changes and a deep acceptance of life as it is. This approach does not mean resignation, but models both thinking and action in a high degree of non-judgemental self-awareness. "You abstract from a specific activity and come into contact with yourself, which results in:

- a reunion of the physical and emotional awareness: You are inside your body rather than are your body
- increasing empathy for yourself and the world around you

Actions based on mindfulness occur mainly in one's consciousness, which does not mean that you have to accept everything that you experience in your life" (Chemi, 2009d). When in negative circumstances, a person can react mindfully in different ways:

1. You can move
2. You can change the situation
3. You can accept the situation

Mindfulness is very easy to use and a very useful tool, but despite its straightforwardness, it should be understood, trained and used personally before it is used in the school or in the classroom. It is recommended that teachers who are interested in mindfulness personally experience and explore mindfulness before they start to function as a mindfulness trainer to their pupils. There are examples of mindfulness exercises for children and young people (see Greco & Hayes, 2008).

The Raisin Exercise

Among the many mindfulness exercises that children and young people can use, I believe that the raisin exercise is excellent in engaging children in a sensory, easily understandable and fun way. The exercise does not need to take a lot of time. Ten minutes is enough time to do the exercise and move the children's attention to a meditative state. The aim of the exercise is to focus attention on a very simple everyday action - to eat and in such a way that this action is experienced in a new, mindful way. The quality of the instructions that introduce the

The Raisin Exercise - continued

exercise are crucial: The teacher should invite the pupils into a mindful state with only a few, manageable sentences and remember that practice makes perfect. To begin with, the children may find the exercise embarrassing or childish and a good strategy would be to allow these feelings and get the pupils to accept them.

Possible instructions: In the next ten minutes we are going to concentrate 0n just being present and on focusing our attention on tasting a specific thing. It is very simple. You are going to eat a raisin very slowly, and while you do this, you are going to feel your body, and notice the taste of the raisin in your mouth. If you want to, you can close your eyes, if that helps you to concentrate. All feelings are allowed. All you have to do is be aware of those feelings and continue concentrating without being interrupted. Breathe in deeply and begin to eat the raisin. Feel the texture of the raisin, the taste, the size. Feel it with your tongue, your teeth, the roof of your mouth. And feel your breathing quietly. If thoughts come into your head, then just let them be there, and notice them, and come back to your breathing. When you are ready, you can open your eyes and look around for a moment, before we start the day.

If the teachers choose to try this exercise, it is important that the pupils are given time to get used to the quietness and to reach a meditative state, which is different from their everyday world of tasks and agreements. Stillness between instructions is fundamental. A serious attempt with mindfulness requires regular training over a longer period of time. Because the raisin exercise is so simple and does not require a lot of time, it is the ideal exercise for the first experiment with mindfulness.

Learning in museums

During a qualitative study in 2011-2012, I had the chance of interviewing and observing museum staff members who are in charge of developing and implementing educational offers in Danish museums. As a result of these meetings and of a simultaneous desk-study of museums' educational products, I was able to describe and analyse the case-studies below. It became clear to me that museum learning is caught between two different agendas: On the one hand, the museums need to sustain a constant flow of visitors and customers, on the other hand schools require new ways of engaging learners and stimulating learning performance (Hein, 1998 and Hooper-Greenhill, 2009). In spite of their geographical and content-related closeness, the sampled institutions display a variety of educational offers: Printed materials (children books), drama and role-play, artefacts manipulation, participation-based lectures and web-resources. This required different methodological approaches, which the table below summarises:

Institution and city	Type of institution	Educational offer	Research method
AROS, Aarhus	Art museum	Educational books published and edited by the museum	Text-analysis, ethnographic observation and interviews
Den Gamle By, Aarhus	Historical open-air museum	Educational dramatisations and history	Ethnographic observation and interviews
Moesgård Museum, Aarhus	History and Archaeology museum	Artefacts display and interaction	Ethnographic observation and interviews

AROS, since its opening in the new building in 2004, has paid special attention to the development of educational programmes for children. The design of the new building included a specific workshop room for hands-on educational activities. Workshops are run by professional facilitators with different educational backgrounds, qualifications and experience. All of these facilitators have very loose contracts with the museum. The fact that the educational employees or stakeholders at museums do not have a steady job at the museum means that their contribution is not systematic, and often museums are not be able to retain the expertise gained by these employees. In the course of this study, I observed a guided tour for school children and I analysed the AROS' educational art-books for children. I will focus on the latter. Specifically, the books included in this study are: Maltha, Pedersen & Schmidt, 2007; Pedersen, 2011; Pedersen, 2009; Schmidt & Bak, 2004; Schmidt & Maltha, 2005; Schmidt, Pedersen & Iversen, 2009.

Examples of books for children are widespread and long used by museums. However, some recent books challenge the traditional book-reading strategies by including more and more interactive tasks: From colouring books to activity books the tradition is long established. The kind of activity I notice in international publications, for instance in the Metropolitan Museum of Art's series (Cressy, 2002 and Falken, 2009), prompts in the young readers nuanced viewpoints, curiosity, questions about observations or cultural interpretations, connections among works of art or artefacts and so forth -perhaps at a higher extent than the AROS books. These books for young readers are able to establish a challenging response by asking the readers to look at something particular in order to discover or imagine the bigger picture or asking the reader to reconsider personal opinions or to invite a second look: "What do you see when you look through the hole?", "Do you think you know the answer?", "Perhaps you need to... Look again!" (Falken, 2009) or by inviting the reader in a quest for details and sharpened observation: "Can you find it?" (Cressy, 2002).

Den Gamle By, "the old town", in Aarhus in Denmark, is a privately owned, open-air museum of Danish urban history and culture (1600-1974). According to Sten Rentzhog (2007) this form of museum stimulates a deep, meaningful learning ("know thyself") and the possibility of knowing about the past in its everyday -and thus perhaps easier to relate to- dimension. A visit to the museum is a whole-body experience: Visitors are literally absorbed into the historical settings and walk through well-staged scenes of historical everyday life. In the last five years, these *tableaux* have been made more and more "*vivant*", by hiring and training extras and actors, who inhabit the old town. Visitors might bump into actors performing as real inhabitants, wiping their doorsteps, driving their horse chariot, cooking soup, selling goods and even interacting verbally with the visitors. The actors' activities may also include walking down the streets in historical clothes, or perform real services in the role of bakery assistants or grocery owners, engaging in conversations with visitors, trained in maintain the high level of make-believe. If you happen to ask the bakery clerk whether you can pay by credit card, she will ask you, what a credit card is, "Is it something from your time, madam?" or if you tell them you come from the States, they will act puzzled and ask for more information: "Oh, you mean America!" The living-museum approach has a strong influence on the museum's guided tours and educational programmes. The first ones are offered to regular visitors and schools and consist in a theme-related journey through the old town, while guided by a museum guide (often a history student or student actor) in historical clothes and role. The narrative and performative elements become even more dominating in the dramatised educational programmes, or more interactive in the educational workshop activities.

The educational activity observed in the present study is a hybrid form, which mixes different communication forms under a common theme. A tragic trial of a young girl that occurred in 1813 was staged for a group of students, who acted as the jury and commentators. The students seemed to take the whole experience and the socially relevant nature of the debate very seriously and contributed with original ideas and personal opinions. The students' genuine participation confirms the emotional involvement seen in other applications of theatre and drama to educational environments (Jackson, 1993), which "use history to raise questions about today" (Prammenter, 1993). These forms of dramatisations, based on a specific theme and historical event, are today a widespread tool of engaging students in learning history and reflecting on historical events. Similar programmes can for instance be experienced at Sverresborg in Trondheim, Norway, where the Trøndelag Folk Museum has developed a Theatre-in-education course on an authentic case in which a young girl was found on the street not far from a pharmacy (probably an illicit drink-shop) in the late 1800's. She had obviously been drinking, had probably met some men who had gotten her into the pharmacy and had been raped. "Minda - the girl from the pharmacy" depicts a current issue today and asks the students to take a critical perspective and consider different points of view: Was it her fault?

At Jamtli in Östersund, Sweden the theme confronted in the programme "On the run" is about being a refugee. Using facts, role-play and discussions, "On the run" takes the participant on a shocking journey. The programme was created in collaboration with the Red Cross, Save the Children and the Immigration Service and exposes the situation of asylum seekers, clarifying the rules within the Migration Board's regulatory system. Here the students can literally feel on their skin what it means to be on the run.

The Open Air Museum in Skanzen in Hungary is located 23 km from Budapest. It runs a project where senior students (17-18 years) who visit the museum are divided into groups in order to "inhabit" four different places and identify with four different families with different backgrounds: Anglicans form the Society of the Holy Cross, Catholics, Jews, actors. The students get lodging in their respective housings in the museum and they assume specific roles in families. They even decide what is going to happen. They hold family reunions on various dilemmas, for example: Could the daughter of the Catholic family marry the son of an actor? Back at school, the work is developed further, when the students create fictive historical documents from the family role-playing. This last example demonstrates good synergy between the school and the museum, something that my interviewees wish for but which is not always possible to establish. The managers of the educational programmes at Den Gamle By maintain that the school-museum collaboration is essential to the optimal learning output, but that the extension and frequency of this collaboration is not yet fully satisfying.

Moesgård Museum is a history and archaeology museum in the Aarhus area, better known as the Viking museum. I had been looking at a specific display whose interactive stimuli included playing with artefacts. In contrast to my observations at the other museums, which were targeted specifically to schools, this display is part of the museum's permanent exhibition and is targeted to all visitors, with a specific attention to children and young people.

The display consists of a single room built around an interactive table immersed in a three-meter long Iron-Age wooded boat, with clothing artefacts that visitors can try on, and a smaller niche with audio materials. The relative simplicity of the room allows a variety of interactions: The wooded boat can be crawled on, the dresses tried on, the interactive table's touch screen touched in order to choose the next story, the radio play can be listened to in a darker corner of the room. The playful interaction with the artefact reproductions seemed to generate fun and engagement. Literally, visitors are able to wear historical knowledge on their bodies. This interactive model has been tried internationally in other museums, such as the biggest children's museum in the world, the Children's Museum in Indianapolis, USA, where the thematic exhibition on Egypt in 2012 included the reproduction of an Egyptian house furnished with clothes to wear and kitchen pots to play with. Another similar example is the Eiteljorg Museum in Indianapolis, dedicated to the arts and culture of Native Americans, where in the children's section the young visitors have the opportunity to dress up in mock-up clothes, to ride in a real horse carriage or play with pots. These are only few of the many examples in museums around the world that include physical interaction with real or reproduced artefacts. The learning consequences of this approach are discussed in the following paragraph with help from previous research on artefacts in museums learning (Tishman, 2008). I consider Moesgård Museum's specific use of artefacts for experiential learning purposes as an innovation compared to the generic inclusion of artefacts in museum exhibitions because of its consistent integration with a variety of other devices (video, sound, narratives, visuals) and because of its "please-touch" approach. In Philadelphia, USA, a museum for children, the Please Touch Museum, challenges the museum identity as something to look at, proposing the alternative practice of active, direct sensory experience. Although similar in approach, the Moesgård Museum installation rather draws its inspiration from Enrique Vargas' theatre of the senses. Based in Barcelona, Spain, the Teatro de los sentidos has inspired a Danish performance group, the Carte Blanche, which, in its turn has inspired Moesgård Museum. According to the professionals responsible of the installation, the idea originally was to build a labyrinth of the senses, which could communicate content in a more appealing way involving body and senses. Museumgoers were expected to track down the meaning within a fragmented narrative, in order to stimulate their imagination and fantasy. The sensory-based approach has been so well accepted at the Moesgård Museum that this perspective will be taken in consideration during the upcoming expansion, when a brand new museum building will be constructed.

Learning as participation

"Why is there a party in the woods?" asks a youngster, participating in an AROS educational programme in response to Danish painter Asger Jorn's 1945 painting, *Guganaga* (Schmidt & Bak, 2004, my translation from Danish). The feedback took place in an educational workshop at AROS, and has been collected together with other memorable children's responses to artworks and published in Schmidt and Bak in 2004. The book is part of a broader publishing initiative that AROS has aimed at young visitors, with the purpose of enhancing learning experiences based on the museum collections. While being a traditional educational tool, the book introduces something new in the tradition of printed books: The voices and thoughts of the educational programmes' lead users -the children. The quotes are skilfully chosen among dense statements, that are assertions including several levels of understanding, and are edited next to the photographic reproductions of the museum's artworks, which inspired them. The child's "Why is there a party in the woods?" reveals deep wondering about a specific artwork and a strong narrative: It speaks volumes about the story the child is imagining. The child's interpretation in this case does not need to be close to any cultural standard or shared cultural understanding, but for the editors of the book, it is a way to give voice to a different interpretation of artworks: The children's "always immediate, unconditional and 'alternative' views" (Schmidt & Bak, 2004, my translation from Danish) or "immediate, often surprising and ingenious comments, questions and answers" (Schmidt & Maltha, 2005, my translation from Danish). "Why is there a party in the woods?" is a poetic question that sets focus on the users' perspective.

Following Schwab's commonplaces of education (1969; 1971; 1973) -subject-matter, teacher, students, and milieu (or setting)- as already attempted in Vallance (2007), we can look at the cases described above. To Schwab's categories, I have added a fifth one: Tools.

Students

The museums' educational offers seem to have a specific focus on the users in the above cases. Some of them express it explicitly ("with a starting point on THEM", "participants in the centre") and tend to design their materials and programmes consequently. The AROS's book series, for instance, relies on users' quotes in at least three out of six books published up until now. These books are intended to be inspiration before or after the museum visit. Most of them are designed the same way, including the same kind of materials: Photographic reproductions of chosen artworks in the museum's collection; brief information about the given artworks, such as the name of the artist, title, date, or in case of *Din Bog om BOY* (Your Book on BOY) additional details about the artwork; quotes from children who have participated in the AROS educational workshops and quotes that are related to the given artwork. In some cases, drawings for children constitute the common narrative thread running throughout the artworks.

The inclusion of participants' quotes in the books represents a strong statement at several levels. The museum indicates its users are central to its dissemination; it takes the young visitors' narratives seriously and it promotes a different way of looking at artworks. In *Din Bog om BOY,* the children's perspective is enhanced by questions that are inspired by the artwork and related to the reader's personal life. For instance "BOY sits all still and watches. His eyes are 23 cm wide. The blue in the eye is as big as a little handball ball. How big is your eye?" (Pedersen, 2011). These questions can contribute to bridging the art experience with the young visitor's everyday life, bringing the artworks' extraordinary dimensions down to the scale of the individual child's everyday life. Emotionally, this can generate a sense of connection and safeness.

The emotional dimension in the form of experiential and hands-on learning is also very present in the other cases that were studied. At Den Gamle By, the dramaturgical form of dissemination is the most widely-used. Role-play or dramatisation involves students in a fixed structure that is living and unfolding under their very eyes. Even when direct interactions are not encompassed within the play, the emotional identification has a central role in this kind of educational form. Students are given roles in the play, sometimes they are asked to put on historical clothes and to perform specific tasks. Even when they are spectators, they are presented with a spectator role that is consistent to the play; for instance they might "play" the witnesses at a contested trial with the decisive task of agreeing to, formulating and communicating the final decision and punishment. The fact of being immersed in an historical or archaeological site, together with the role-play activity, can generate a deeper understanding of cultural events or values, together with more interest and engagement. Even though the students' outputs have not been mapped in the present study, the employees responsible for the educational offers who were interviewed, report a great satisfaction with the effect of "different communication forms" on the students.

Relating museums' educational programmes and materials to users' participation and emotions, almost makes common sense, from the perspective of edutainment. When education and entertainment blend, of course users are involved in participative, often interactive, experiences that involve an emotional response of some sort. In the present study, the specific way the institutions achieve this is by means of living voices. This approach to educational or dissemination tools and its emotional outputs will be discussed below, under the section "tools". What I wish to underline now is the fact that included in the living voices are the users' voices, with their own style, their opinions, and their specific narratives. In the case of AROS, these voices were collected by a psychologist, who interviewed children looking at artworks, prompting them with different questions that became the series of books' common theme (Why? What do you think? Perhaps?). In the case of Den Gamle By, the users' voices are not documented but happen "live", with the task and in the middle of the dramaturgical structure. Students are asked to participate while the play unfolds and within the play.

Subject-matter

All of the museums contacted within the present study, both during the preliminary study and the ethnographic interviews, report an active adaptation of their different educational offers to the specific target groups. This means that the great variety of offers is being adapted to the school level of the group that is requesting the museum's services: For instance, the same historical dramatisation at Den Gamle By can be adapted for all ages of secondary school pupils or even teacher students. How the museums adapt their educational programmes to developmental levels is something this study was not able to reveal: The museum employees are vague in their answers when this question is being asked, and tend not to answer directly. Studies in this field, based on systematic observation on how this adaptation is done, would be highly needed. Ørngreen & Levinsen point to at least at three tendencies (2009):

1. Adaptation of educational material to the specific school level.
2. Loose adaptation to the students' age level, by means of teacher's guides.
3. "One size fits all" solution.

Looking at the above from a learning perspective, it is noticeable that either the adaptation happens by adopting the school criteria fully in a one-to-one correspondence between schools national targets and teaching materials, or by not really facing any pedagogical or educational consideration about developmental levels. The former approach delivers detailed descriptions of what to do and how to do it in the class or at the museum location, looking at the teacher's resources not as a guide or inspiration, but as a strict instruction manual. While this might save the teachers considerable preparation time, making them more willing to include a museum learning experience in the school curriculum, it might also backfire on them. The more strict a teacher guide is, the less freedom and creativity the teacher may experience, with serious consequences for the teacher's involvement in and ownership for the teaching session. So, on one hand the first model could be positive because it saved time, on the other hand it might affect the teacher's creativity and ownership. Secondly, the strict adherence to schools national targets can only be done by excluding content that is not contemplated by school programmes. This has an immediate consequence on the museums' overall approach to educational content: Is the objective of the museum supposed to be that it is provides learning as a supplement to the school's ordinary level curriculum, or should its objective be to provide learning that is much more original than what is provided by the school? At the moment, museums seem to contribute to learning either by offering ordinary school content in a different, sensory based and experiential way, or by offering unique information, knowledge or sources, which would otherwise be excluded by the school's curriculum. The ordinary approach, more common among museums (according to Ørngreen & Levinsen, 2009, p. 12), gives different learning styles and experiential learning experiences the opportunity to unfold. The extra-ordinary approach widens both the teachers' and students' knowledge horizons, by means of "very specific subjects, which make possible in teaching to include perspectives, which would otherwise be difficult to find, with the same body of details and collected material" (Ørngreen & Levinsen, 2009, p. 12, my translation from Danish).

However, in addition to the school-focused approach, I noticed a different attitude towards learning objectives. Two of my cases have expressed an understanding of the learning outcomes they can offer as broader educational development (*Bildung*) and inspirational experience. "We should not teach them anything *about* art, we must inspire them; it is about one's self and open eyes", says one of the museum employees, showing a clear distinction between mode 1, learning *about* something, and mode 2, learning *in* the task (Barnett, 2004). To Barnett's categories, I add a fourth mode, learning *through* a task or tool, but neither this nor Barnett's mode 3, dealing with hyper-complexity, has been mentioned or dealt with in the observed cases.

Teacher

"Teachers" in museums and historical sites can be several individuals with different roles. During specific educational programmes, we can meet the following educator roles:

1 Schoolteachers escorting their pupils through specific educational programmes offered by the museums.
2 Museum educators or employees that are in charge of the teaching or content dissemination.
3 Parents or adults in general guiding children during non-structured visits.

The teacher role, no matter who of the above is involved, acquires a different meaning at the museum location. The role of the educator as "mediator" is verbalised at AROS, as the one who gives children the keys for a cultural encounter. This implies, for instance, that at AROS what is most important within educational programmes is the educational employees' attitude: He/she must be empathic and respectful in the meeting with other people, and must be excited about the subject matter, which is going to be disseminated. Educators assume the function of role models within a given culture: They can transmit knowledge, skills, tools, but also passion and appreciation.

Regarding the active application of learning theories in practice, the museum case-study has encountered a great deal of diversity. In this respect, I observed three different approaches:

1 Full integration of theories in educational practices.
2 Theories are not applied to educational practices.
3 Statement of application of the theories to educational practices but in actuality, they are neglected.

When the first occurs, educational employees tend to produce their own theory-based materials and disseminate the theory/practice-bridge to other educators. This is for instance the case of Den Gamle By, where the model in Figure 15 has been developed and it is actively used as educational material in order to introduce other educators to the dramatised and experiential approach at the museum location, or as theoretical background understanding in the development of educational programmes and activities at the open-air museum. However, it must be underlined that the employees' have a mixed professional background, drawn both from formal teacher education, formal drama and theatrical practices. This double function allows the two main employees to navigate successfully in both worlds, having a deep understanding for the school teachers' needs (school content and objectives), the students' attention triggers and the overall pedagogical considerations to achieve optimal learning. At Den Gamle By, they do not talk about teaching, but about dissemination and historical upbringing.

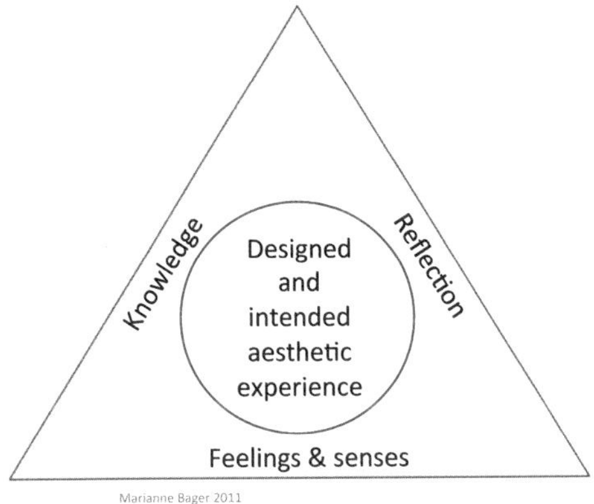

Figure 15 Aesthetic learning processes at Den Gamle By (adapted from Bager, 2011, my translation)

Only one of the materials analysed includes any mention of other kinds of educators in a school or museum: Parents or adults escorting children in museum visits. It is almost an incidental footnote, but in our context very meaningful. In a final acknowledgment note, Schmidt & Bak mention the participating children's responses to artworks, which "have prevented their art interested parents to fall into habitual ways of thinking and traditional art appreciation" (2004). Parents in the role of guides and learning brokers should be more systematically considered in museum learning experiences.

Tools

The museums visited during this study show a wide variety of educational offers. I will describe now the common thread in the tools observed in this study's cases. All of them make use of complex messages, which stimulate the students cognitively and living voices, which enhance emotional responses.

complexity → cognitive intensity
living voices → positive emotions

The complexity, if not hyper-complexity, of the educational offers can be described as a multimodal text, often setting the stage for interaction, collaboration and participation. Let us take the above-described exhibition at Moesgård Museum, where sound, videos and artefacts all contribute to a total experience. The visitor is literally immersed in history, their bodies are inside the historical artefact and their minds are kept busy trying to decode all of the different stimuli happening at the same time. AROS builds complexity in its books by means of informed choices about the artworks that are reproduced, about the children's quotes, about accompanying illustrations or texts. All of the books that were analysed, display artworks that are complex in their own right: That is, artworks that are not immediately or intuitively decoded, but rather need a high level of cognitive engagement. These artworks are hard nuts to crack because they are ambiguous, they can be interpreted in several ways and at different levels, they are dense with meaning and techniques, and often they present enigmas that make viewers wonder. The complexity of the artworks is then echoed by the children's quotes and the narrative structure in the books. The children's quotes mirror the same quality of the artworks: They are chosen among the statements that show deep thinking and the activation of imaginative and narrative skills. For instance "Why did the children run away?" is the quote in response to Jens Ferdinand Willumsen's painting depicting three middle-aged men in a living room, sitting in armchairs and listening to one of them who is reading from a book. The living room looks quite empty and the child formulating the question has apparently noticed what is missing from the picture, coherently to the story she imagined. The children's questioning make visible complex thoughts inspired by the artworks (and by the adult guidance in looking at the artworks). Concerning the complexity in the book structure, mentioned above, it is constructed by merging illustrations with their own independent narrative to the classic structure of art books. In doing so, the books from the AROS series for children include the following elements: Pictures of complex artworks, short facts on artworks (often just name of artist, title and date), children's quotes, and illustrations. The latter have the look of illustrations for children's books and have both an independent narrative that can be followed regardless the artworks, and a commentary related to the artwork, reproduced on the same page. These illustrations work as a visual translation into children's visual imagination and provide the young readers with an interpretive key. Looking at the illustrations the child might feel safe in the meeting with the unknown artwork, they look familiar, harmless and most of all they have a structure the child can recognise and decode. The logic of the illustrations follows the same logic of children's books (age 0-9): They present a funny character (animal, child), the drawings looks like a cartoon, and the characters do funny things with humour.

Even though none of the observed tools have a specific focus on stimulating or documenting participants' deep thinking, all of them seem to shape many opportunities for challenging cognitive tasks. In this case, there is room for improvement for the future.

Regarding the emotional side of the museum learning experience, the following elements have been observed in the design of educational tools:

- Emotional participant response
- Multi-senses perception
- Sensory richness and complexity
- Narratives
- Bodily experiences

In the Moesgård Museum case with artefacts, for instance, the body is immersed in a complex learning environment, by the visitor putting on historical clothes or sitting on the Viking boat. Visitors are allowed and expected to touch the artefacts and conquer the space. The environment is dynamic, surprising, and kinaesthetic. The same bodily-immersive experience characterises the visits at Den Gamle By, where visitors have a whole town and many outdoor spaces to approach the experience physically (incidentally, according to one of the museum educators, this is perhaps what makes this historical site so popular among "*specialklasser*" (classes for students with special needs). Attention to the emotional side of the museum experience is cultivated in the appealing to the body, the senses and, last but not least, by means of living voices. In all of the educational offers considered in the present study, developers have included the possibility of listening to a living narrative or of telling one's own story. What I define as living voices are to be found in Den Gamle By's dramaturgical experiences, in AROS' children's quotes, in Moesgård Museum's multimodal narrative. In all the cases, a voice tells a story from its viewpoint, with a specific way of telling and an emotional fascination. Cultural content becomes personal, accessible and to be related to. When the educator/actor interprets a real historical character, he/she is communicating a wide range of emotional messages together with the content or school-related subject matter. When students are asked to play along, they contribute with their voice and opinions. The children's voice is integrated into the art book with the abrupt and spontaneous style of a children's narrative. While the visitor discovers details about Viking history, a narrator voice tells a story of a battle and background noises cause us to make imaginative associations. These voices are alive and make the museum a living environment, opening up to a different kind of learning, which is embodied, sensory-based, experiential and closely related to the individual's cultural and existential understanding.

Milieu (or setting)

In the museum case study, the examples take educational design into consideration and build a specific learning environment, where non-formal, informal and formal elements coexist within the same educational activity. What is characteristic is the non or informality of the setting, together with the formality of educational purpose and aims, which makes this learning environment something in between the two domains of formality/non-formality. In these environments, all of the educational tools seem to be sensory-rich, and emotionally and cognitively challenging. The learning they intend to achieve is approached and defined differently, but I did not encounter a specific focus on the learning potential of cultural mediators, such as the arts or artefacts, and awareness about learning and documentation of deep thinking (Ritchhart, 2007). The museum educators in this case-study have an empathic, pedagogical aware, playful and content-related approach to the educational programmes and materials they develop, and their main focus tends to be on the user's experience and the expected positive outputs.

A few specific concerns arise out of the present case study: The first is that museums could end up designing educational programmes driven exclusively by schools expectations. The museums' need for funding and high visitor numbers might have a negative influence on their design of learning environments. They might value pleasing visitors more than learning outcomes or providing high-quality experience. Museums can entertain, but they also provide supplementary or alternative documentation to learning: They can provide the strongest support to formal learning environments by means of cognitive puzzles, physical involvement, interaction, sensory stimuli and emotions. The other concern is about the diversity of educational offers encountered. On the one hand, diversity and plurality are advantages for sales and for holding interest levels high, on the other hand experiments that are not always necessarily evidence-based or documented and communicated to the field of peers, might damage more than they reward. A paradigm-shift in the direction of a thoughtful integration of museums' culture and pedagogy in schools might require stronger qualitative evidence, focused on learning outputs and benefits, and this would call for further, large-scale qualitative research.

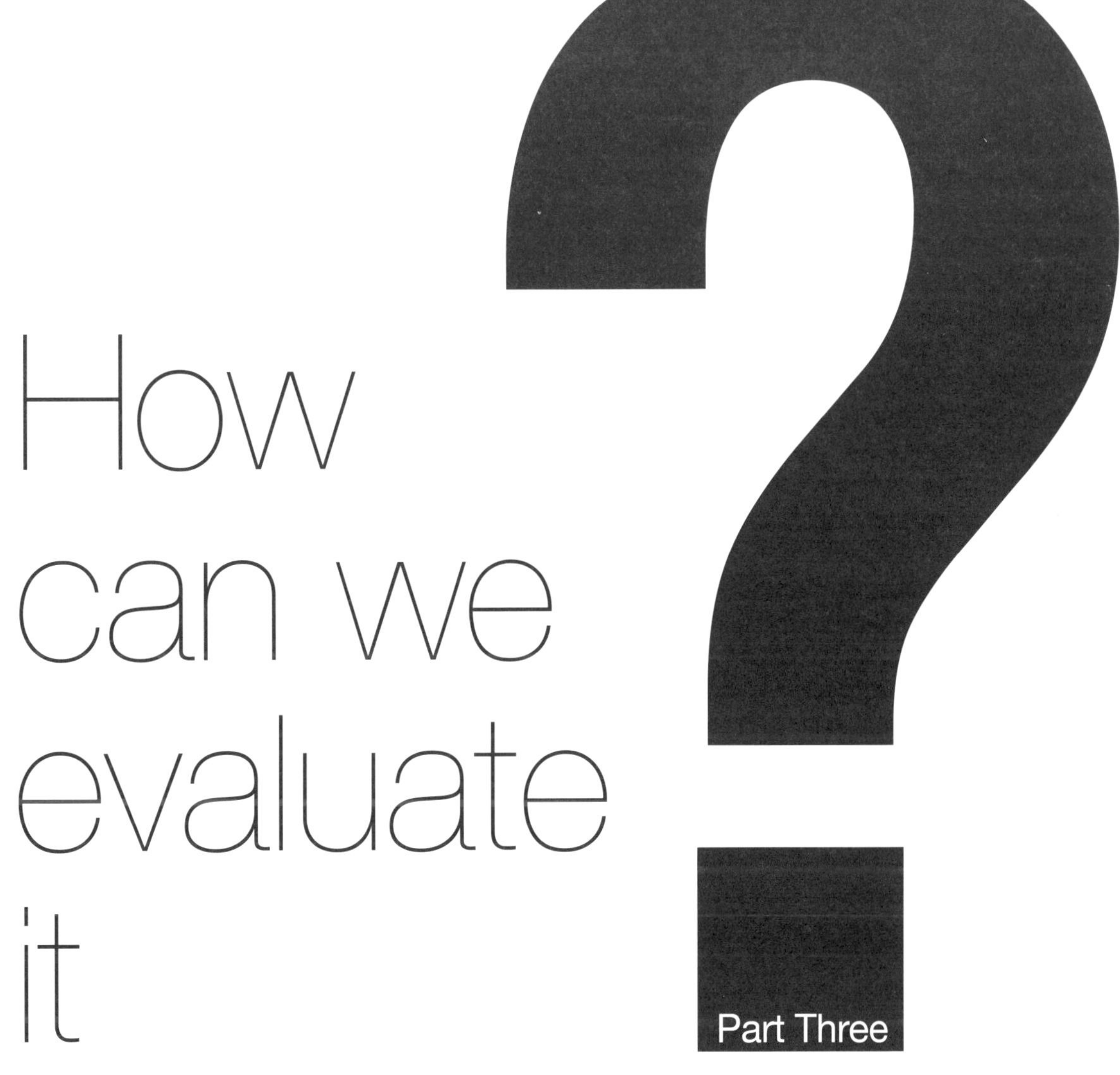
How
can we
evaluate
it
?
Part Three

Theoretical perspectives

When someone loves art, there is no occupation that is more boring than mine. But when someone creates art, there is no occupation that is looked up to more than mine. My job is to remove all of the magic from artworks and explain the hidden meanings, symbols, allusions, values, procedures, compositions, criteria, etc. As an individual who is able to explain a joke, I am trapped between two opposites: On the one hand, the pedagogic urge to analyse and disseminate the artistic content and on the other hand, accept the respect for the sensory, aesthetic, physical attraction in the art. The former is my professional background: culture studies, the analysis of literature, performance and visual arts and answer the equivalent to the humourless task of explaining a joke. The latter represents my fascination with art, of the artistic processes and learning process and in the joke's metaphorical answer to a good delivery of a quip that does not have to be explained.

My awareness of this schism has followed me since a good friend and literary author admired my ability to analyse an artwork and my role as a disseminator of culture: "To write a book is the easiest thing. But what you are doing, explaining literature to the profane it's the most difficult job. And important".

With this in mind, I will now introduce some of my research tools: Theories and methods. My aim is to give the reader the opportunity to continue with their own studies in the field with some applied theoretical and methodological considerations.

The scientific theory that formed the background for this study has been strongly inspired by John Dewey's pragmatism and learning theory (Dewey, 1963 and 2005; Jackson, 1998). Dewey's progressive pedagogy is the primarily framework of understanding that is used here. Eclectic by nature, pragmatism plays an important role in the modern idea of pedagogy, educational studies and art. I find pragmatism particularly useful for this study because of the selected field (school) and the research field (art). I believe that a pragmatic approach is better when used with a context-specific field, which school, learning and art can be because it is able to "capture" the elements determined by the context.

Even though research topics in schools can be thematised as generalisable, for example in a statistical study about how many children skip school, the school as an environment is naturally related to context. Learning situations cannot be separated from their social, cultural or ideological context. Therefore, qualitative studies are often used in school settings. Dewey's pragmatism ensures a scientific realisation of the school's context-specificness: "Experience doesn't happen in a vacuum" (Dewey, 1963, p. 40), but when it happens, it is experienced and understood in a given context. According to Dewey "Experience" forms the background for learning, particularly high-quality learning. Children acquire new knowledge through good experiences and direct experiences, their deep learning can be transformed into experiences in and of the real world.

The aesthetic and artistic learning processes are experiences, which are determined by context, just as all of the cognitive activities are, and to a greater degree than other types of learning. Elliot Eisner defined beautifully the "experience of environment" as a "process that is shaped by culture, influenced by language, impacted by beliefs, affected by values, and moderated by the distinctive features of that part of ourselves we sometime describe as our individuality" (Eisner 2002, p. 1). The sensory system and cognition are culturally determined because they do not exist by themselves but within a context: "[The] sensory system doesn't work alone in a vacuum, but in a cultural context" (Eisner, 2002, p. 2).

Dewey's theories can be integrated with Vygotsky's cultural heritage approach (Connery, John-Steiner & Marjanovic-Shane, 2010) and with Gardner's theory on multiple intelligences (Gardner, 1994). The awareness that these theoretical approaches share that we learn differently and that all children have specific strengths and talents is a fundamental element of the framework of understanding for the MMALP project described earlier. In the Artfulness study, I have focused on the aesthetic, physical, playful and artistic ways to learn, however, I do not regard this as excluding the logical, mathematical and linguistic. Even though in this book the artistic learning processes are the main theme, they emphasise the learning theories I refer to, in a clear, integrated approach. Despite this fact, we should still advocate for a specific perspective on and understanding of the artistic processes and theories. My approach has therefore been to, on the one hand, examine a professional knowledge of the characteristics of artistic processes and on the other hand, observe the interface between these processes and other types of learning and thinking.

Gardner's theories have inspired several research efforts in the direction that is reported here: Artistic learning processes. These studies are admirable excellent examples of research-based development and development-based research: *The Visible Thinking* and *The Artful Thinkin*g are frameworks of understanding representing Gardner, and Goodman's theories (Goodman, 1976). A specific perspective is used among these frameworks of undertaking: The research-based framework Cultures of Thinking and its associated "cultural forces", which are the areas that research has pointed out as crucial with regard to creating optimal learning processes (Ritchhart, 2002).

The artfulness study's theoretical approach leans towards the abovenamed theoretical perspectives, especially in the understanding of learning as being social, relational and context-related and as a complex and comprehensive cognitive process. That is, learning in this study should not be understood as good grades or the ability to pass an exam but as the ability or disposition to think and to reflect. In addition, this approach is associated with a positive psychological understanding for positive emotions and their relation to learning and creativity.

As regards to content, this summative account has a specific focus on creativity and aesthetic and artistic approaches. This means that a substantial review of creative theories and aesthetic-theoretical approaches have been explored and studied (Kaufman & Sternberg, 2010). The preferred creativity theory approach is Csikszentmihalyi (1996).

POSITIVE PSYCHOLOGY

Is a psychological orientation that looks at the optimal sides of human flourishing rather than diagnostic and medical conditions, as traditional psychology have a tendency to. Its purpose is to contribute to human development with evidence-based knowledge and research.

A second meta-theoretical framework that I use is positive psychology, in particular its focus on positive emotions, positivity and flow in learning (Csikszentmihalyi, 2000; Fredrickson, 2009).

In recent years, the positive psychological direction has contributed to research-based knowledge about positivity, which is used here. Flow theory and creativity theory fall within these research-related interests, which are brought together in Csikszentmihalyi's sharp contribution (1990, 1996, 2000) and special views on art (Csikszentmihalyi & Robinson, 1990).

Positive psychology researchers and neuroscientists know that feeling and emotions are interrelated with cognition in general and with learning situations in particular. Experiencing positive emotions is the basic prerequisite and output for excellent learning processes. The learner learns best when he/she feels comfortable, secure, adequately challenged, happy and if they experience meaning in what they are doing. The good life (hedonistic gratification), the engaged life (flow state) and the meaningful life (to belong, to look forward to something, to be of significance for someone else) are the cornerstones for a life that cultivates a positive state.

Within positivity, this book has particular focus on flow states and flow experiences during teaching and learning. Flow is by definition a positive state of concentration (Csikszentmihalyi, 2000) and very desirable in schools, because:

- It is a positive state that can be experienced as well-being.
- It is a state of concentration and therefore a sign of a high level of engagement.

The flow theory is well-suited to building a bridge between learning and the child's experience (Csikszentmihalyi, 1996, 2000). According to the theory, an individual has a good chance for experiencing a positive state

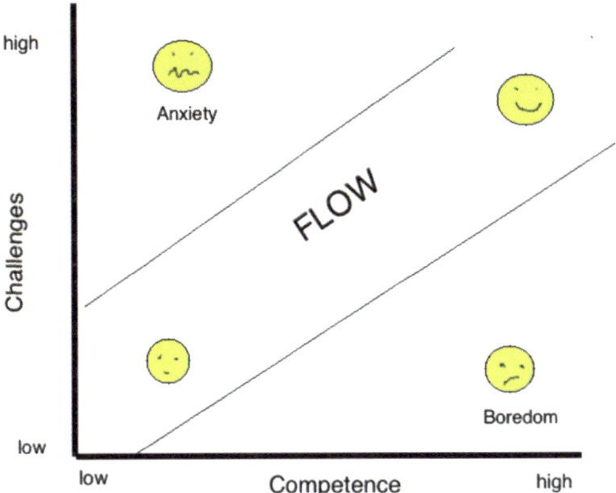

Figure 16 Flow model inspired by Csikszentmihalyi, 1990

of deep concentration in a given activity when the individual's competencies correspond sufficiently to the degree of difficulty of the task. The positive function of sufficiently adjusted challenges is meticulously emphasised in the Flow Theory (Csikszentmihalyi, 1990, 2000), where excellent learning and creativity are linked to effort, which is evolutionary-psychologically based (we are "programmed" to work hard to survive) and rewarded by our brains. Research shows that the flow state generates positive neuron transmitters' chemicals in the brain that increase our attention and which is a very positive experience. This helps to create good conditions for creative learning, because positive work and learning conditions strengthen memory, create new ideas, thoughts, associations and are experienced as being very meaningful. The experience of meaningfulness actively strengthens engagement and the falling away of self-awareness and therefore activates flow, which at a biological level is experienced as increased levels of dopamine and positive neurotransmitter chemicals in the brain.

This theory has its obvious application in teaching, where it can be applied to both explain (the teachers interpret the children's teaching output) and normative objectives (the teachers plan the teaching by designing a project that generates the best opportunities for achieving a flow state).

Taking the flow model shown above as the point of departure, it can be said that a pupil with a high level of competency in a specific subject or topic also requires a high level of academic challenging. If the child cannot be stimulated optimally, he or she will become bored, or if the child is challenged excessively, he or she will experience anxiety and fear. The research shows that a good balance between the task's challenges and the individual's competencies is an important prerequisite for learning, whereby a high level of flow can be an excellent indication of learning.

These theoretical approaches function as a whole, in that on the one hand learning is perceived as basically experience-based and on the other hand as covered by the specific relationship between positive emotions and cognitive intensity within these experiences. The reader will note that the informants' statements, which are quoted in this book, are divided into *emotional outcome*, which is understood in the light of the positive psychological approach to positive emotions and the *intellectual-academic output*, which is understood on the basis of the cognitive approach. This division though is fictive and purely answers the analytical need of understanding these phenomena scientifically. In reality, this book makes the point of non-separation of the two areas: Emotions and cognition, artistic and academic subjects are (and can be) integrated. As a framework of understanding in the data collection in the Artfulness study, I have taken inspiration from phenomenology, where focus is on the people: Phenomenology provides a basic examination of how phenomena actually turn out. This view has inspired and has been applied actively in my field observations and my interaction with the informants.

Inspiration for your own (re)search

For specific inspiration, I can give an account of the methodological strategies I have used during the Artfulness research project, which is described in Chemi, 2011 (pp. 20-31).

When a teacher or educator wants to examine something that is research related, he or she can choose to formulate a research question (or several) or to relate openly to the research field. In the Artfulness project, I had already formulated the areas that I was interested in examining, and I had the following questions as the focal point:

- Are there examples of art-based educational programmes in Danish schools?
- What are their most important characteristics?
- What are the strengths and needs in this area?
- Can Artfulness contribute to creating a culture of deep thinking and engaging learning in Danish schools?
- Which future prototypes of an optimal creative school can the Danish teachers' envisage?

My interest was based on a specific theoretical background, which I deepened with ad hoc literature and contributions and at the same time I prepared the empirical part of my research.

The process, which consists of the selection of the subject area, i.e. the place that is to be examined/observed, is called the sampling process. Within the Artfulness study, the participating schools were selected as part of the sampling process in several stages, and which covered the whole municipality. The sampling process took the form of a mapping of all of the schools in the municipality, which was carried out in October-November 2009, where I examined the schools' interests in an active involvement in the aesthetic and artistic learning processes. The sampling process was structured the following way: 1. Telephone interview with the school leader, 2. Collection of responses, 3. Grouping responses in thematic categories, 4. Selection of the schools whose interests or activities demonstrated a link between artistic craftsmanship and reflection (which was the link I was particularly interested in observing). The telephone interviews were prepared by devising an interview template, i.e. a guide for the interview that could help me maintain focus on my central points of interest. My interview template was characterised by an introduction where I presented myself as a researcher for the MMALP project, and gave a short description of my project and asked the following questions:

- Does your school have special projects/courses for art in teaching or does it use art in cross-disciplinary collaboration?
- Does your school place special focus on the aesthetic/artistic learning processes?
- Is there one or more teachers at your school who are particularly engaged in art and aesthetics?

My objective was to let the schools define whether they had a special focus, interest, activity or staff engaged in my research field. Out of 35 schools, some of the schools gave a definitive no, others were unsure what I meant by the aesthetic and artistic learning processes and started a positive dialogue with me, which sometimes ended with a negative response ("we do not have focus on the aesthetic learning processes") or a positive response with reservations: 15 schools gave a positive response and some with great excitement. This enthusiasm opened up a positive professional dialogue about art and aesthetics in the school, where the informants described their approach at the school. Subsequently, I divided the data I had into three categories: Large projects, smaller projects and projects that lacked clarification. I was interested in the large projects, which extended beyond general teaching or the school curriculum and within the group of large projects there were six projects that the school leaders defined as a link between art and reflection. It was from this angle that I would study, so the six schools were invited to join in a research collaboration.

Before beginning a field observation or carrying out interviews, it is advisable that the researcher ensures there is an alignment of expectations and the research project's purpose and design is clarified. This phase covers a number of ethical principles that should always be in focus when the research concerns people. For example, in MMALP all of the researchers were aware of this. The guidelines that we followed were the guidelines that are applied to every social study: Anonymity, clear agreements, ongoing information, security and respect (see Knoop et al., 2009, pp. 19-20) and at the same time the research quality must meet excellent scientific standards. In this regard, it would be appropriate to develop research in accordance with the Danish Agency for Science, Technology and Innovation (Recommended Guidelines for

Research Ethics in the Social Sciences, 2002, my translation), which points out the following requirements:

1. The researcher must consider to what degree the research project is compatible with **excellent scientific standards**. The researcher must also consider whether the dependence of one kind of another can affect the research work contrary to academic or ethical principles.

2. It is the responsibility of the social researcher to carry out research in **consideration** of the people and groups that are the subject of the research and with other groups who may be affected by the research work and its results. The researcher must avoid causing unnecessary difficulty and disadvantage or unnecessarily infringing other people's privacy.

3. The researcher is responsible for ensuring that the **information** that is collected or made available for research does not come into the hands of an unauthorised person, in a form that makes it possible to identify the people who are the subject of the research or have contributed to the research work.

4. It is the responsibility of the researcher to acquire **consent** from the people who are involved in the research. The individuals in question must be informed that participation is voluntary.

5. It is the responsibility of the researcher to make the results of the research available to the public and to submit them in accordance with standard scientific principles and avoid distorted or incomplete presentations.

Specifically within Artfulness, the participating schools were invited to collaborate and informed of the project's purpose, overall design and duration beforehand, and informed of the researcher's expectations of their role and contribution to the project. A declaration of intent, an informed consent and a letter to the selected schools was sent out before the field work commenced. After positive feedback from the schools, the Artfulness' empirical collection phase was officially started.

As further documentation for the ethical responsibility in the research work, the teachers that were involved in the reported cases were given the opportunity to read through their quotes and comment on the text. This was done to validate the researcher's understanding and to provide the teachers who had agreed to participate with names, the opportunity to make their opinions known.

With regards to the pupils, I chose to publicise all of their quotes or contributions in an anonymous form, which also applies to this book. All of the pictures of the pupils in the report were reproduced with the permission of parents and of the schools.

A final comment with respect to the research method concerns the researcher's role in the field. Even though the chosen methodological approach contemplates discreet observations and as little interaction with the subject matter as possible, it was often the case that the presence of the researcher was reported as having a positive influence on the study's participants. The educators and teachers from the Artfulness project felt that my presence as a researcher attached to the observed projects had been rewarding and positive. The involved parties account of the dialogue with me as a researcher shows that they saw my function as being very positive, inspirational and a rewarding way to exchange and discuss ideas.

At one school, a pupil even reported that she got help from the researcher by mentioning my name together with the other observers, even though I had deliberately kept myself outside of the artistic and pedagogic activities in the classroom. The child's experience of the researcher's presence as being positive assistance is noteworthy and together with the teachers' feedback about the positive and rewarding exchange and discussion of ideas, it is evidence of a positive and energising and secure influence on the subject matter from the researcher.

It is not possible to say whether my presence as a researcher or external observer has had any impact on the research results since my study has not had any specific focus on this part of the research process. But despite the fact that a specific effect cannot be determined, the children's and teachers' statements document clearly a positive experience in regards to the collaboration with the researcher.

Observers should therefore be aware that under all circumstances, their presence will affect the research field.

After these considerations and stages, the more active part of the research process can begin, i.e. the phase where data is collected: Field observations and interviews.

There are many ways to collect empirical data, for example:

- Ethnographic observations and field notes
- Video documentation
- Interviews can be:
  - Structured: The Researcher decides beforehand, which questions shall be asked and prepares an interview protocol. This type of interview can also be carried out in writing, in the form of a qualitative questionnaire, i.e. a questionnaire that allows personal expressions or views.
  - Semi-structured: The Researcher prepares an interview protocol beforehand, which may be changed. This protocol differs from the structured one in that it is more of guideline and a source of inspiration rather than a fixed script.
- Focus group interviews
- Actions research
- Questionnaires can be:
  - Quantitative
  - Qualitative

When the teacher or educator has collected the data (transcripts of interviews, video recordings, filed notes, etc.), the analysis can begin. It will be an advantage if the resear-

Questionnaires: How to form questions.

Quantitative

Question: "Do you sleep well at night?"
Answer: "yes/no/don't know"

or

Statement: "I sleep well at night"
Answer: "strongly agree/agree/disagree/strongly disagree/don't know"

or

Question: "How do you sleep at night?"
Answer: "very well/well/poorly/very poorly/don't know"

Result: Statistic of the collected responses.

Qualitative

Question: "How would you describe your sleep at night?" or "How well do you sleep at night?"

Answer: (a personal response)

Text analysis

Online resource: http://textalyser.net

cher has some expertise in analytical methods (e.g. text or discourse analysis) or if not, they can collaborate with experts who can help with these methods. Open source software that can be used to analyse text is also readily available. These tools can help to highlight key words and find patterns in the texts. There is also literature available online that demonstrates how to carry out an analysis for uncovering interesting patterns. These patterns or deviations are the research results, or so-called findings.

This process is slow and creative and often chaotic and frustrating. It will be very helpful if several advisors or supervisors or informal assistants are found who can support this process.

The final part of a research process is the dissemination of the results. All of the results are useful to the research community, especially when taken from well-designed and well-run research. The research results that come from the teacher-researcher or educator-researcher or a collaboration between the researchers and the teachers, has enormous importance because they are descriptions or insights that experts working in the field have generated. I would like to see more of these enterprises from "practitioners" or many more collaborations between "practitioners" and "theorists", possibly based on an action research design, whose aim is to create deep dialogue between cultures and deep understanding.

This democratic research approach and a more systematic attention to innovation initiatives in education can help to establish a pedagogic culture that vales and supports optimal and creative learning through assessment.

Among the research methods that are used in the schools and institutions, action research has been very successful (Reason & Bradbury, 2001).

Action research is an action-oriented research method based on *an active collaboration between the practitioners and the professional researchers.* This means that the practitioners at the educational institutions are recognised as experts in their fields who are also able and entitled to explore their practice autonomously. The practitioners can in this perspective, either independently start reflections, metareflections and research projects or choose to enter into collaboration with professional researchers. This collaboration may be intended to create a joint forum for the purpose of defining the issues that shall be examined and create relevant knowledge about the issues, learn and research social research techniques, make action-oriented decisions and interpret what the participants have learned (Martin, 2001, p. 201).

Action research distinguishes itself from the different methods that are used in social research because of its focus on creating shared learning, new and deep insights and concrete changes.

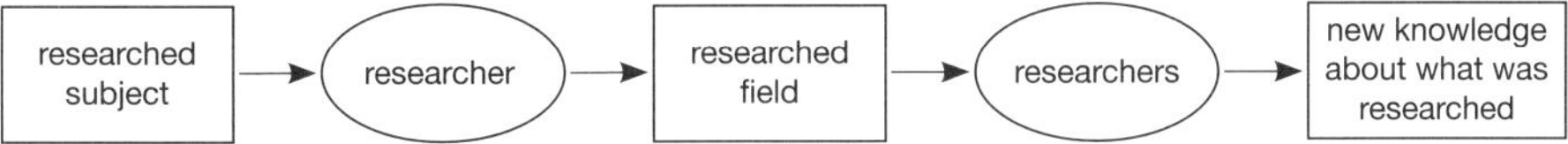

Figure 17 Traditional relationship researcher-field

Many research designs have a tendency to separate the experts and practitioners in a linear process that divides the two parties into different roles: The researchers collect the knowledge in the researched field and disseminate it among researchers.

In contrast, an action research approach ensures that the practitioners have a great deal of influence on the research process and on the de-

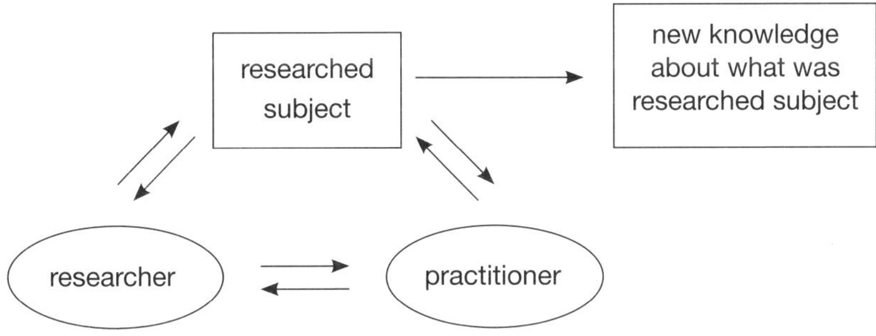

Figure 18 Relationships within action research

velopment process. If they wish to, the practitioners can also develop independent studies without the researcher. In action research, the relations between the participants and the research is more interactive, democratic, engaging and prone to create ownership of the evaluation process. In this way, the practitioners bring all of their knowledge into play with the benefit of a relevant reflection, documentation and evaluation.

The roots of action research in schools can be traced back to the 40s and 50s, when Stephen Corey, head of the Horace Mann-Lincoln Institute for School Experimentation at Columbia University, decided to do something about the gap between theory and practice in classroom research. Corey "believed that teachers would make better decisions in the classroom if they conducted research to determine the basis for their decisions" (Zeichner, 2001, p. 274). Over time, action research spread to the UK and Australia, so that today we can describe it as a special Anglo-Saxon school culture, which considers teachers as independent researchers, defined as *teaching as scholarship*. This term refers to a reflective and meta-reflective dimension in teaching practice, which can be actively used to generate new insight and research. The research design is in this case based on the following elements: Planning, actions, observations and reflections in teaching.

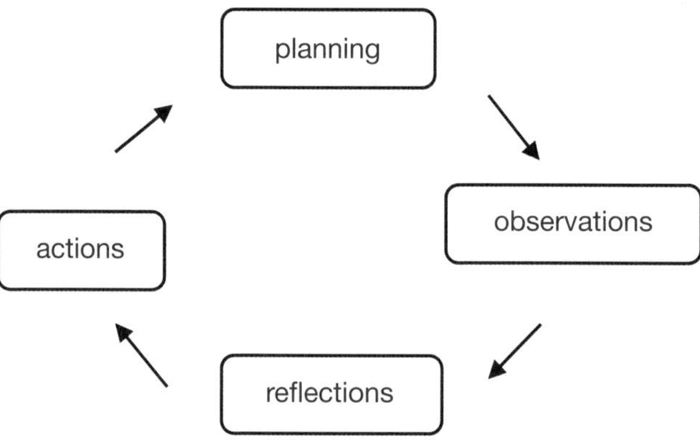

Figure 19 Teaching as scholarship

Action research in practice

Should teachers want to practise (meta) refection with help from action research, they can start by asking themselves and their colleagues research questions that are most used within action research in schools. In general, they belong to the following categories:

- Improvement of practise: How can I stimulate my pupils to be more creative?
- Better understanding of a particular aspect of practice: Can my teaching engage my pupils optimally? How can I have an impact on my students?
- Better understanding of uniform practice in general: What happens in the class when I use learning styles?
- Improved fairness: How can I help bilingual pupils, so that they have self-esteem and are on an equal footing with the others?
- Influence on the social dimension of practice: How can I convince the decision-makers to redistribute resources so that the tasks in teaching comply with the resources at the schools?

Cases

By way of providing concrete examples of the use of action research in teaching, I will use two fictive but very realistic cases: A top-down case and a bottom-up case.

- Top-down

Imagine a medium-sized municipality realises that there is a pressing need to improve the school environment. To this purpose, it establishes an ambitious project that involves all of the participants in the educational system within the municipality – politicians, school leaders, teachers, educators and pupils. These participants are actively involved together with a group of professional researchers in an action research programme.

The participants, who have clear and strong political support, start a number of dialogic and participatory processes: Large group processes (see Martin 2001), dialogue conferences (see Pålshaugen 2001), and a number of development projects for the purpose of testing different ways to learn and to teach. Several networks and study groups are formed, which will discuss shared experiences and interpret individual observations and experiences.

The researchers facilitate the process and ensure that they coordinate the broad picture that emerges. The results are jointly disseminated on several levels: The researchers and practitioners publish scientific articles in collaboration.

- Bottom-up

This is the more usual case in action research, which typically involves the practitioners themselves, who initiate the process.

A group of teachers notice that the girls in the class are not engaged and lack motivation. A negative synergy develops where the girls distance themselves from the daily lessons in the classroom. The teachers realise they need to study the phenomenon to better understand it. They have spoken with their school leader but there are no available funds to pay for a training course. The teachers decide to set up their own small research unit in the form of a study group and they begin to note down their observations in a log book and at the same time learn more about action research.

Via an online study, the teachers come into contact with an international network, which focuses on their selected issue. The teachers develop their research independently, without help from professional academics and publish several academic articles about their findings. (from Chemi, 2009f).

References

Adorno, Theodor W. (1997). *Aesthetic Theory*. Minneapolis: University of Minnesota Press (I 1970).

Amabile, T. M. (1996). *Creativity in context: Update to the Social Psychology of Creativity*. Boulder: Westview Press.

Andersen, Frans Ørsted. (2008). *Flow i "Overvågningens dilemma" – Forskningsrapport fra en projektuge i 9.kl*. December 2008. Aarhus: Møllevangskolen.

Aristotle. (2009). *The Poetics*. The Project Gutenberg EBook. Oxford: The Clarendon Press (I ed. 1920).

Arnheim, Rudolf. (1997). *Visual Thinking*. Berkeley: University of California Press (I 1969).

Austin, Robert & Devin, Lee. (2003). *Artful Making: What Managers Need to Know About How Artists Work*. New York: Pearson Education.

Austring, Bennyé D. & Sørensen, Merete. (2006). *Æstetik og læring: grundbog om æstetiske læreprocesser*. København: Hans Reitzels Forlag.

Bager, Marianne. (2011). *Formidling i Den Gamle Bys Undervisningsafdeling og Levende Museum*. Aarhus: Den Gamle By.

Bamford, Anne. (2006). *The Wow Factor: Global Research Compendium on the Impact of the Arts in Education*. New York, Waxmann.

Bamford, Anne & Qvortrup, Matt. (2006). *The Ildsjæl in the Classroom: A Review of Danish Arts Education in the Folkeskole*. Kunstrådet. (April 2006).

Bang, Silas. (2010). Peitersens malebog er vigtig læring. In: *Vejle Amts Folkeblad*, (1st June 2010).

Barnett, R. (2004). Learning for an unknown future. *Higher Education Research and Development.* 23(3). 247 – 260.

Ben-Sahar, Tal. (2007). *Happier. Learn the Secrets to Daily Joy and Lasting Fulfilment*. New York: McGraw Hill.

Ben-Sahar, Tal. (2009). *The Pursuit of Perfect. How to Stop Chasing Perfection and Start Living a RICHER, HAPPIER Life*. New York: McGraw Hill.

Berger, Ron. (2003). *An Ethic of Excellence: Building a Culture of Craftsmanship with Students*. Heinemann.

Brown, N. J. L., Sokal, A. D., & Friedman, H. L. (2013). The complex dynamics of wishful thinking: The critical positivity ratio. *American Psychologist*, 68(9): 801-813.

Bruner, Jerome. (1973). Going beyond the information given. In: Anglin, J. (ed.). *Beyond the Information Given*, pp. 218-238. New York: Norton.

Catterall, James. (2009). *Doing Well and Doing Good by Doing Art*. Los Angeles and London: Imagination group/I-Group Books.

Chemi, Tatiana. (2006). *Artbased Approaches: A Practical Notebook to Creativity at Work*. Fokus Forlag.

Chemi, Tatiana. (2008). Kunst og organisatorisk kreativitet og innovation. In: *Kognition og Pædagogik: Tidsskrift om Gode Læringsmiljøer*, 18(69): 54-75.

Chemi, Tatiana. (2009a). *Artfulness* i skolen: nydelse og læring for livet. In: Brinkmann, Svend & Tanggaard, Lene (eds.). *Kreativitetsfremmende læringsmiljøer i skolen*. Frederikshavn: Dafolo.

Chemi, Tatiana. (2009b). *KDH - Kunst Design Håndværk: Et Folkeskoleforsøg. Forskningsrapport fra et projektforløb i 4.-5.kl., januar-juni 2009, Engum Skole, Vejle*. Retrieved 4th June 2014. In: www.universefonden.dk/lib/file.aspx?fileID=200&target=blank.

Chemi, Tatiana. (2009c). Artfulness. Retrieved 24th November 2010. In: www.blivklog.dk/page12934.aspx?searchString=artfulness.

Chemi, Tatiana. (2009d). Mindfulness. Retrieved 11th Maj 2011. In: www.blivklog.dk/page13017.aspx?searchString=mindfulness.

Chemi, Tatiana. (2009e). The Future of Learning Institute: Globalisering, digitalisering og hjerneforskning. In: *Kognition og Pædagogik: Tidsskrift om Gode Læringsmiljøer*. Virum: Dansk Psykologisk Forlag, 19(74): 42-55.

Chemi, Tatiana. (2009f). Aktionsforskning. Retrieved 11th Maj 2011. In: www.blivklog.dk/page13076.aspx.

Chemi, Tatiana. (2010a). *Animationsværksted: integration af kreative og boglige fag i undervisning. Forskningsrapport fra et projektforløb i 2. kl., marts-maj 2010, Nørup Skole, Vejle*. Retrieved 4th June 2014. In: www.universefonden.dk/lib/file.aspx?fileID=201&target=blank.

Chemi, Tatiana. (2010b). *Malerens malebog: inddragelse af eksperter og lokalsamfund i undervisning. Forskningsrapport fra et projektforløb for hele skolen, januar-juni 2010, Andkær Skole, Vejle.* Retrieved 4th June 2014. In: www.universefonden.dk/lib/file.aspx?fileID=202&target=blank.

Chemi, Tatiana. (2010c). Hvad betyder det at undervise i design i folkeskolen. In: *Håndarbejde i skolen*, 4(November 2010): 6-9.

Chemi, Tatiana. (2010d). Artfulness i læring og undervisning: et forskningsprojekt om kreativitet og æstetiske læreprocesser. In: *Undervisere*. UN9(September 2010). Retrieved 24th November 2010. In: www.undervisere.dk/ObjectOtherShowExtra.aspx?objectId=64138.

Chemi, Tatiana. (2010e). The Artful school as Optimal Experience and Learning. Paper presented at the European Conference on Positive Psychology, Copenhagen, 23rd-26th June 2010. Retrieved 24th November 2010. In: www.universeresearchlab.dk/page12739.aspx.

Chemi, Tatiana. (2011). *Artfulness i Vejle: Forskningsrapport fra et kvalitativt studie i folkeskoler, 2009-2010, Vejle Kommune*. Februar 2011. Retrieved 4th June 2014. In: www.universefonden.dk/lib/file.aspx?fileID=207&target=blank.

Chemi, Tatiana. (2012). Performancestudier. In: Frans Ørsted Andersen og Gerd Christensen (Eds.) *Den positive psykologis metoder – forskning, assessment, test, udviklingsarbejde og intervention* (pp. 57-85). Dansk Psykologisk Forlag.

Chemi, Tatiana. (2013). Performancestudier. In: Frans Ørsted Andersen og Gerd Christensen (Eds.) *Den positive psykologiens metoder - Forskning, kartlegging, testing, utviklingsarbeid og intervensjon* (pp. 54-78). Oslo: Gyldendal.

Chemi, Tatiana. (2014). The Artful Teacher: A Conceptual Model for Arts Integration in Schools. In: *Studies in Art Education*, (Fall 2014).

Chemi, Tatiana & Kastberg, Peter. (in press). Education Through Theatre: Typologies of Science Theatre. In: *Applied Theatre Researcher*, in press.

Chemi, Tatiana, Jensen, Julie Borup & Hersted, Lone. (in press). *Behind the Scenes of Artistic Creativity: Processes of Learning, Creating and Organising*. New York: Peter Lang, in press.

Collins, M. A., & Amabile, T. M. (1999). Motivation and creativity. In: R. J. Sternberg (Ed.), *Handbook of Creativity* (pp. 297-314). Cambridge: Cambridge University Press.

Collins, Allan & Halverson, Richard. (2009). *Rethinking Education in the Age of Technology: the Digital Revolution and the Schools*. New York: Teachers College Press.

Corbin, Juliet & Staruss, Anselm. (2008). *Basics of Qualitative Research*. SAGE.

Cressy, Judith. (2002). *Can You Find It?* New York: Abrams Books for Young Readers.

Csikszentmihalyi, Mihaly. (1990). *Flow: The Psychology of the Optimal Experience*. New York: HarperCollins.

Csikszentmihalyi, Mihaly. (1996). *Creativity: Flow and the Psychology of Discovery and Invention*. London: HarperCollins.

Csikszentmihalyi, Mihaly. (2000). *Beyond Boredom and Anxiety: Experiencing Flow in Work and Play*. San Francisco: Jossey-Bass (I 1975).

Csikszentmihalyi, Mihaly & Robinson, Rick E. (1990). *The Art of Seeing: An Interpretation of the Aesthetic Encounter*. Los Angeles: Paul Getty Museum.

Csikszentmihalyi, Mihaly & Schiefele, Ulrich. (1992). Arts Education, Human Development, and the Quality of Experience. In: Reimer, Bennet & Smith, Ralph A. (eds.). *The Arts, Education, and Aesthetic Knowing*, pp. 169-191. Chicago: The University of Chicago Press.

Damasio, Antonio R. (1994). *Descartes' Error: Emotion, Reason, And The Human Brain*. New York: Putnam.

Damon, William. (1984). Peer education: The untapped potential. In: *Journal of Applied Developmental Psychology*, 5(4): 331-343.

Darsø, Lotte. (2004). *Artful Creation: Learning-Tales of Arts-in-Business*. Frederiksberg: Samfundslitteratur.

Davis, Jessica & Gardner, Howard. (1992). The Cognitive Revolution: Consequences for the Understanding and Education of the Child as Artist. In: Reimer, Bennet & Smith, Ralph A. (eds.). *The Arts, Education, and Aesthetic Knowing*, pp. 92-123. Chicago: The University of Chicago Press.

De Bono, Edward. (2000). *Six thinking hats*. London: Penguin.

Denzin, Norman & Lincoln, Yvonna S. (eds.). (2005). *The Sage Handbook of Qualitative Research*. Thousand Oaks: SAGE.

De Petrillo, Lili & Winner, Ellen. (2005). Does Art Improve Mood? A Test of a Key Assumption Underlying Art Therapy. In: *Art Therapy: Journal of the American Therapy Association*, 22 (4): 205-212.

Dewey, John. (1963). *Experience and Education*. New York: Macmillan (I 1938).

Dewey, John. (2005). *Art as Experience*. London: Perigee (I 1934).

Dissanayake, Ellen. (1995). *Homo Aestheticus. Where Art Comes From and Why*. Seattle and London: University of Washington Press (I 1992).

Dissanayake, Ellen. (2000). *Art and Intimacy: How the Art Began*. Seattle and London: University of Washington Press.

Education for All: Global Monitoring Report. (2011). *The Hidden Crisis: Armed Conflict and Education*. UNESCO. Retrieved 20th June 2011. In: http://unesdoc.unesco.org/images/0019/001907/190743e.pdf.

Eisner, Elliot W. (2002). *The Arts and the Creation of Mind*. New Haver & London: Yale University Press.

European Union. (2009). *European ambassadors for creativity and innovation.* Retrieved 12th February 2014. In: www.create2009.europa.eu/fileadmin/Content/Downloads/PDF/Manifesto/manifesto.en.pdf

Eriksen, Mette. (2009). Fint med forsker-øjne. In: *Vejle Amts Folkeblad*, (16th January 2009).

Falken, Linda C. (2009). *Look Again!* London: Thames & Hudson.

Forsknings- og Innovationsstyrelsen. (2002).*Vejledende retningslinjer for forskningsetik i samfundsvidenskaberne*. Retrieved 4th March 2011. In: www.fi.dk/publikationer/2002/vejledende-retningslinier-for-forskningsetik-i-samfundsviden/ssf-etik.pdf.

Fredrickson, Barbara L. (1998). What Good Are Positive Emotions? In: *Review of General Psychology*. Educational Publishing Foundation, 2(3): 304-306.

Fredrickson, Barbara L. (2009). *Positivity: Groundbreaking research reveals how to embrace the hidden strength of positive emotions, overcome negativity, and thrive*. New York: Crown.

Fredrickson, B. L. (2013). Updated thinking on positivity ratios. *American Psychologist*.

Fredrickson, Barbara L. & Branigan, Christine. (2005). Positive emotion broaden the scope of attention and thought-action repertoires. In: *Cognition and Emotion*. Psychology Press, 19(3): 313-332.

Friedman, Victor J. (2001). Action Science: Creating Communities of Inquiry in Communities of Practice. In: Reasons, Peter & Bradbury, Hilary (eds.). *Handbook of Action Research: Participative Inquiry and Practice*, pp. 159-170. London: SAGE Publications.

Gardner, Howard. (1993). *Creating Minds: An Anatomy of Creativity Seen Through the Lives of Freud, Einstein, Picasso, Stravinsky, Eliot, Graham, and Gandhi*. New York: Basic Books.

Gardner, Howard. (1994). *Frames of Mind. The Theory of Multiple Intelligences*. London: HarperCollins (I 1993).

Gardner, Howard. (2003). *Multiple intelligences: the theory in practice*. New York: BasicBooks.

Gardner, Howard & Davis, Katie. (2013). *The App Generation. How Today's Youth Navigate Identity, Intimacy. And Imagination in a Digital World*. New Haven and London: Yale University Press.

Glover, John A., Ronning, Royce R. & Reynolds, Cecil R. (eds.). (1989). *Handbook of Creativity*. New York and London: Plenum press.

Goldie, Peter. (2002). *The Emotions: A Philosophical Exploration*. New York: Oxford University Press.

Goleman, Daniel. (1997). *Emotional Intelligence: Why It Can Matter More Than IQ*. Bantam Books (I 1990).
Goodman, Nelson. (1976). *Languages of Art: An Approach to a Theory of Symbols*. Indianapolis/Cambridge: Hackett Publishing Company.
Greco, Laurie A. & Hayes, Steven C. (eds.). (2008). *Acceptance & mindfulness treatments for children & adolescents: a practitioner's guide*. Oakland: New Harbinger Publications.
Harrison, Charles & Wood, Paul (eds.). (1992). *Art in Theory. 1900-2000: An Anthology of Changing Ideas*. Blackwell.
Harrison, Charles, Wood, Paul & Gaiger, Jason (eds.). (1998). *Art in Theory. 1815-1900: An Anthology of Changing Ideas*. Blackwell.
Hein, George. (1998). *Learning in the Museum*. London: Routledge.
Hetland, Lois, Winner, Ellen & al. (2007). *Studio Thinking: The Real Benefits of Visual Arts Education*. New York and London: Teachers College Press.
Hooper-Greenhill, Eilean. (2009). *Museums and Education: Purpose, Pedagogy, Performance*. London: Routledge.
Huizinga, Johan. (1955). *Homo ludens: a study of the play-element in culture*. Boston: Beacon Press.
Illeris, Knud (Ed.). (2009). *Contemporary Theories of Learning: learning Theorists... in their Own Words*. London and New York: Routledge.
Immordino-Yang, Mary Helen & Damasio, Antonio. (2007). We Feel, Therefore We Learn: The Relevance of Affective and Social Neuroscience to Education. In: *Journal Compilation*. International Mind, Brain, and Education Society and Blackwell Publishing. 1(1). 3-10.
Immordino-Yang, Mary Helen & Fischer, Kurt W. (2009). Neuroscience bases of learning. In: Aukrust, V. G. (ed.). *International Encyclopedia of Education: Section on Learning and Cognition*. Oxford: Elsevier.
Isaacson, Walter. (2011). *Steve Jobs*. London: Little, Brown.
Jackson, Philip. (1998). *John Dewey and the Lessons of Art*. New Haven and London: Yale University Press.
Jackson, Tony (ed.). (1993). *Learning Through Theatre: New Perspectives on Theatre in Education*. New York and London: Routledge.
Jensen, Julie Borup. (2011). Working with Arts in Nurse Education. In: *Designs for Learning*, 1(4): 34-47.

Johnson, Burke R. & Onwuegbuzie, Anthony J. (2004). Mixed Methods Research: A Research Paradigm Whose Time Has Come. In: *Educational Researcher*, 33(7): 14-26.

Johnstone, Keith. (1996). *Impro: Improvisation and the Theatre*. Methuen.

Journal of Aesthetic Education. (2000). *Special Issue. The Arts and Academic Achievement: What the Evidence Shows*, 34(3/4): 2-90.

Kabat-Zinn, J. (1990). *Full Catastrophe Living: How to cope with stress, pain and illness using mindfulness meditation*. New York: Hyperion.

Kabat-Zinn, J. (1994). *Wherever you go, there you are: Mindfulness meditation for everyday life*. Westport: Hyperion.

Kahneman, D. (2011). *Thinking, Fast and Slow*. London: Penguin.

Kaufman, J. C., & Sternberg, R. J. (2010). In: Kaufman J. C. (Ed.), *The Cambridge Handbook of Creativity.* New York: Cambridge University Press.

Kemmis, Stephen & McTaggart, Robin. (2005). Participatory Action Research: Communicative Action and the Public Sphere. In: Denzin, Norman & Lincoln, Yvonna S. (eds.). *The Sage Handbook of Qualitative Research*, pp. 559-603. Thousand Oaks: SAGE.

King, Ian & Vickery, Jonathan. (2013). *Experiencing Organisations: New Aesthetic Perspectives*. Faringdon: Libri Publishing.

Knill, Paolo, Levine, Ellen G. & Levine, Stephen K. (2005). *Principles and Practice of Expressive Arts Therapy: Toward a Therapeutic Aesthetics*. London and Philadelphia: Jessica Kingsley Publisher (I ed. 2004).

Knoop, Hans Henrik. (2002). *Play, Learning and Creativity: Why Happy Children Are Better Learners*. Copenhagen: Aschehoug.

Knoop, Hans Henrik et al. (2009). *Et forskningsbaseret udviklingssamarbejde mellem Vejle Kommune og Universe Research Lab: 1. Rapport*. Retrieved 4th June 2014. In: www.universefonden.dk/lib/file.aspx?fileID=198&target=blank.

Knoop, Hans Henrik et al. (2010). *Mmalp midtvejs i projektet: Midtvejsstatus, november 2010*. Retrieved 4th June 2014. In: www.universefonden.dk/lib/file.aspx?fileID=199&target=blank.

Knoop, Hans Henrik et al. (2011). *Et forskningsbaseret udviklingssamarbejde mellem Vejle Kommune og Universe Research Lab: 3. Rap-*

port. Retieved 4th June 2014. In: www.universefonden.dk/lib/file.aspx?fileID=208&target=blank.

Knowles, Gary J & Cole, Andra L. (eds). (2008). *Handbook of the Arts in Qualitative Research*. Los Angeles and London: SAGE.

Krejberg, Gunvor Ganer, Kastberg, Peter & Chemi, Tatiana. (2010). Videnskabsteatret – teaterformatet i naturvidenskabens tjeneste. *Chara. Tidsskrift for kreativitet, spontaneitet og læring*, *1*: 87-116. Retieved 30th March 2011. In: www.chara.dk/udgivelser/201001/artikler/20100109.pdf

Langer, Ellen J. (1993). A Mindful Education. In: *Educational Psychologist*, 28(1 January 1993): 43-50.

Langer, Ellen. (1997). *The Power of Mindful Learning*. Cambridge: Merloyd Lawrence Book.

Langer, Ellen. (2006). *On Becoming an Artist*. New York: Ballantine Books.

Levitin, Daniel J. (2006). *This is Your Brain on Music: the Science of a Human Obsession*. New York: Plume.

Luthar, S. S. (2006). Resilience in development: A synthesis of research across five decades. In: Cicchetti, Dante & Cohen, Donald J. (ed.), (2006). Developmental psychopathology, Vol 3: Risk, disorder, and adaptation (2nd ed.), (pp. 739-795). Hoboken, NJ, US: John Wiley & Sons Inc, xvi, 944 pp.

Maltha, Peter, Pedersen, Birgit & Schmidt, Finn Lykke. (2007). *Hvad tror du? En børnebog om kalkmalerier*. Aarhus: Klim.

Martin, Ann L. (2001). Large-group Processes as Action Research. In: Reasons, Peter & Bradbury, Hilary (eds.). *Handbook of Action Research: Participative Inquiry and Practice*. London: SAGE Publications. 200-208.

Maslow, A. H. (1943). A Theory of Human Motivation. In: *Psychological Review*. 50. 370-396.

Murray, Chris (ed.). (2003). *Key Writers on Art: The Twentieth Century*. London and New York: Routledge.

Nakamura, Jeanne & Shernoff, David. (2009). *Good Mentoring: Fostering Excellent Practice in Higher Education*. San Francisco: Jossey-Bass.

Pålshaugen, Øyvind. (2001). The Use of Words: Improving Enterprises by Improving their Conversations. In: Reasons, Peter & Bradbury,

Hilary (eds.). *Handbook of Action Research: Participative Inquiry and Practice*, pp. 209-218. London: SAGE Publications.

Pavis, Patrice. (2003). *Analyzing Performance: Theatre, Dance and Film*. Ann Arbor: University of Michigan Press (I 1996).

Pedersen, Birgit. (2011). *Din bog om BOY*. ARoS.

Pedersen, Birgit & Jensen, Louis. (2009). *Stygge sterger. En kunstbog for børn*. Klemantis.

Pennac, Daniel. (2010). *School Blues*. London: Maclehose Press.

Perkins, David N. (1992a). *Outsmarting IQ: The Emerging Science of Learnable Intelligence*. Simon & Schuster.

Perkins, David N. (1992b). *Smart Schools: From Training Memories to Educating Minds*. New York: The Free Press.

Perkins, David N. (1994). *The Intelligent Eye: Learning to Think by Looking at Art*. Los Angeles: Paul Getty Trust.

Perkins, David N. (2009). *Making Learning Whole: How Seven Principles of Teaching Can Transform Education*. San Francisco: Jossey Bass.

Prammenter, David. (1993). Devising for TIE (53-70). In: Jackson, Tony (ed.). (1993). *Learning Through Theatre: New Perspectives on Theatre in Education*. New York and London: Routledge.

Rahman, F. (2014). We Are Not All Malala. *Wired Citizenship: Youth Learning and Activism in the Middle East,* 153.

Reasons, Peter & Bradbury, Hilary (eds.). (2001). *Handbook of Action Research: Participative Inquiry and Practice*. London: SAGE Publications.

Reimer, Bennet. (1992). What Knowledge Is of Most Worth in the Arts? In: Reimer, Bennet & Smith, Ralph A. (eds.). *The Arts, Education, and Aesthetic Knowing*, pp. 20-50. Chicago: The University of Chicago Press.

Reimer, Bennet & Smith A. Ralph. (1992). *The Arts, Education, and Aesthetic Knowing*. Chicago: University of Chicago Press.

Rentzhog, Sten. (2007). *Open-air Museums: the History and Future of a Visionary Idea*. Östersund: Jamtli.

Ritchhart, Ron. (2002). *Intellectual Character: What it is, Why it Matters, and How to Get it*. Jossey-Bass Education.

Ritchhart, Ron. (2007). Cultivating a Culture of Thinking in Museums. In: *Journal of Museum Education*, 32(2): 137-154.

Ritchhart, Ron & Perkins, David. (2000). Life in the Mindful Classroom: Nurturing the Disposition of Mindfulness. In: *Journal for Social Issues*, 56(1): 27-47.

Ritchhart, Ron & Perkins, David. (2008). Making Thinking Visible. In: *Educational Leadership*, 65(5): 57-61.

Ritchhart, Ron, Palmer, Patricia, Church, Mark & Tishman, Shari. (2006). *Thinking Routines: Establishing Patterns of Thinking in the Classroom*. Paper prepared for the AERA Conference, Harvard Graduate School of Education, (April 2006). Retrieved 5th December 2011. In: www.pz.harvard.edu/Research/AERA06ThinkingRoutines.pdf.

Robinson, Ken. (2001). *Out of Our Minds: Learning to be Creative*. Chichester: Capstone.

Robinson, Ken. (2009). *The Element: How Finding Your Passion Changes Everything*. London: Penguin.

Robinson, Ken. (2011). Educating the Creative Mind. *Lego Idea Conference*. Conference lecture. Billund (14th April 2011).

Rotne, Nikolaj Flor & Rotne, Diddi Flor. (2011). *Mindfulness i pædagogikken*. København: Hans Reitzels Forlag.

Salomon, Gavriel & Globerson, Tamar. (1987). Skill May Not Be Enough: The Role of Mindfulness in Learning and Transfer. *International Journal of Educational Research*, 11(6): 623-37.

Schein, Edgar E. (1992). Organizational Culture and Leadership. San Francisco: Jossey-Bass.

Schmidt, Finn Lykke & Bak, Mette-Kirstine. (2004). *Hvorfor? En kunstbog for børn og barnelige sjæle*. Aarhus: Klim.

Schmidt, Finn Lykke & Maltha, Peter. (2005). *Måske? En kunstbog for dyr, børn og barnelige sjæle*. Aarhus: Klim.

Schmidt, Finn Lykke, Pedersen, Birgit & Iversen, Bo Odgård. (2009). *Skvulp. En kunstbog for børn om skulpturer og installationer*. Aarhus: Klim.

Schwab, J. (1969). The practical: A language for curriculum. *School Review*, 75(1), 1-23.

Schwab, J. (1971). The practical: Arts of the eclectic. *School Review*, 79(4), 493-542.

Schwab, J. (1973). The practical: Translation into curriculum. *School Review*, 81(4), 501-522.

Seldin, Peter. (2004). *The teaching portfolio: a practical guide to improved performance and promotion/tenure decisions*. Bolton: Anker Pub. Co.

Seligman, M. E. P. (2002). *Authentic Happiness*. New York: Free Press.

Shernoff, David. J. & Csikszentmihalyi, Mihalyi. (2008). Flow in schools: Cultivating engaged learners and optimal learning environments. In: R. Gilman, E. S. Heubner, & M. Furlong (eds.), *Handbook of Positive Psychology in the Schools*, pp. 131-145. Mahwah, NJ: Erlbaum.

Spencer, Herbert. (1966). *On Education*. New York: teachers College Press, Columbia University.

Spolin, Viola. (2000). *Improvisation for the Theatre*. Evanston: Northwestern University Press.

Spradley, J.P & McCurdy, D.W. (1972). *The Cultural Experience: Ethnography in Complex Society*. Prospect Heights: Waveland.

Starko, A. J. (2001). *Creativity in the classroom: Schools of curious delight* (2nd ed.). Mahwah: Lawrence Erlbaum.

Taylor, Steven. (2012). *Leadership Craft, Leadership Art*. New York: Palgrave Macmillan.

Tishman, Shari. (2008). The Object of Their Attention. *Educational Leadership*. 65(5). 44-46.

Tishman, Shari & Andrade, Albert. *Thinking Dispositions: A review of current theories, practices, and issues*. Retrieved 16th December 2010. In: http://learnweb.harvard.edu/alps/thinking/docs/Dispositions.htm.

Tishman, Shari & Palmer, Patricia. (2006). *Artful Thinking: Stronger Thinking and Learning through the Power of Art. Final Report Submitted to Traverse City Area Public Schools*, (November 2006). Cambridge: Project Zero.

Tishman, Shari & Palmer, Patricia. (2007). Works of Art Are Good Things to Think About. In: *Evaluating the Impact of Arts and Cultural Education*, pp. 89-101. Paris.

Turner, Victor. (1967). *The Forest of Symbols*. New York: Cornell University Press.

Undervisningsministeriet. (2009). *Kreative fag bliver prøvefag som forsøg*. Retrieved 13th March 2009. In: www.uvm.dk/Uddannelse/Folkeskolen/Om%20folkeskolen/Nyheder/Folkeskolen/Udd/Folke/2009/Marts/090313%20Kreative%20fag%20bliver%20proevefag%20som%20forsoeg.aspx.

Vallance, Elizabeth. (2007). Questions Asked in Art-museum Education Research (700-716). In: Bresler, Liora (ed.). *International Handbook of Research in Arts Education*. Springer.

Vecchi, V. (2010). *Art and creativity in Reggio Emilia: Exploring the role and potential of ateliers in early childhood education*. New York: Routledge.

Visible Thinking. (2009). *Visible Thinking Resource Book*. Cambridge: President and Fellow of Harvard College.

Webb. N.M. (2010). *Peer Learning in the Classroom*. Retrieved 16th December 2010. In: www.sciencedirect.com/science/referenceworks/9780080448947.

Webster. (1989). *Webster's Encyclopedic Unabridged Dictionary of the English Language*. New York: Gramercy Books (I 1983).

Wickström, G & Bendix, T. (2000). The Hawthorne effect: what did the original Hawthorne studies actually show? In: *Scandinavian Journal of Work, Environment & Health*, (26)4: 363-367.

Winner, Ellen. (1982). *Invented Worlds: The Psychology of the Arts*. Cambridge and London: Harvard University Press.

Yousafzai, M., & Lamb, C. (2013). In Yousafzai M. (Ed.), *I am Malala: The girl who stood up for education and was shot by the taliban.* New York: Little Brown and Company.

Zeichner, Ken. (2001). Educational Action Research. In: Reasons, Peter & Bradbury, Hilary (eds.). *Handbook of Action Research: Participative Inquiry and Practice*, pp. 273-283. London: SAGE Publications.

Zinder, David. (2002). *Body Voice Imagination: A Training for the Actor*. New York and London: Routledge.

Ørngreen, Rikke & Levinsen, Karin Tweddell. (2009). *E-museum: evaluering af digitale undervisningsmaterialer*. School of Education, University of Aarhus.

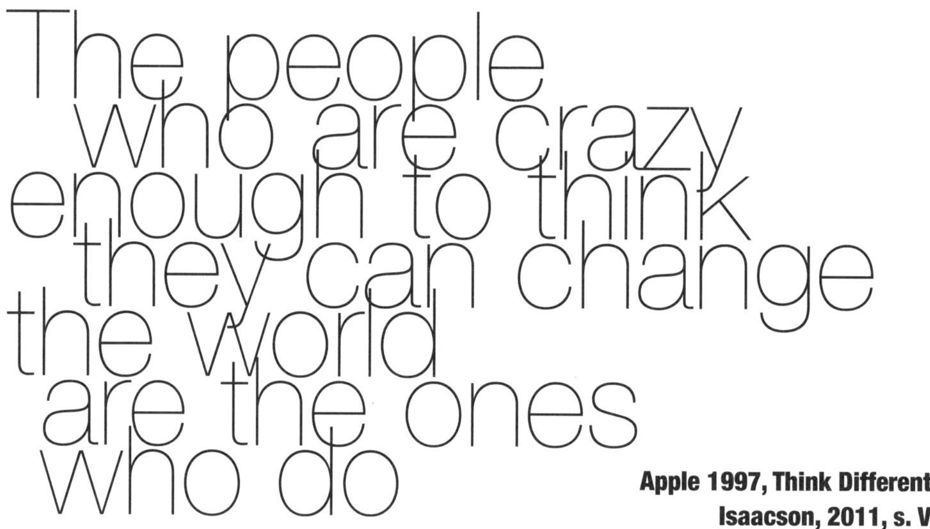

Apple 1997, Think Different
Isaacson, 2011, s. V

About the author

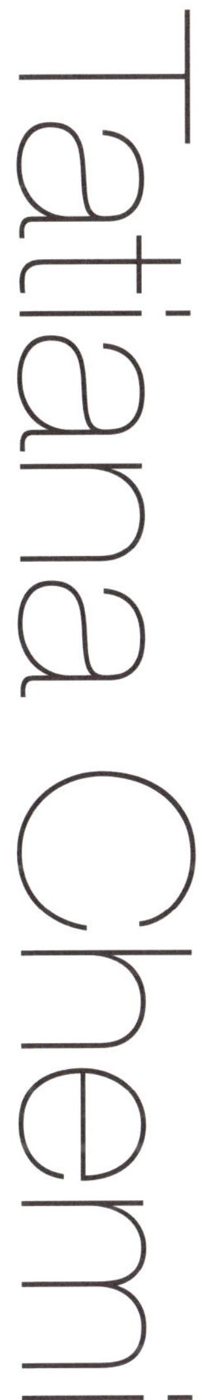

Tatiana Chemi, PhD is Associate Professor at Aalborg University, Chair of Educational Innovation, where she works in the field of artistic learning and creative processes, a field that she specifically focused on during Post Doc research at the Danish School of Education (DPU). As a graduate in Italian Literature and Theatre, with a PhD in Contemporary Theatre History, she has a deep understanding of aesthetics and artistic practices. She has been a senior researcher at Universe Foundation and researcher at Universe Research Lab; a teaching assistant for the Dept. of Dramaturgy at the University of Aarhus and lecturer of History of World Literature and Visual Arts at the Scandinavian Department of the Russian Theatre School GITIS. She has organised and led several cultural projects, including the international theatre meeting *The Multicultural Space* (Denmark 1-9 May 2002) and the Samuel Beckett Centenary in Denmark (November 2006), where she made her debut as a theatre director with the play *Come and Go*. Currently, she participates in the following research groups: ARiEL (Arts in Education and Learning, co-founder and leader), FIU (Research in Education and Cultures of Learning), HERG (Higher education research group). At the research centre reCreate (Research Centre for Creative and Immersive Learning Environments) she has the roles of Coordinator of junior researchers and Coordinator of publishing strategy. She is the author of many published articles and reports, and is also the author of *Artbased Approaches. A Practical Handbook to Creativity at Work*, Fokus Forlag, 2006, and *Kunsten at integrere kunst i undervisning* [The art of integrating the arts in education], Aalborg Universitetsforlag, 2012 and *In the Beginning Was the Pun: Comedy and Humour in Samuel Beckett's Theatre*, Aalborg University Press, 2013. In 2013, Aalborg University Press named her Author of the Year. She is currently involved in several research projects examining artistic creativity, arts-integrated educational designs in schools and the role of emotions in learning. She is Italian, a yoga enthusiast and excellent cook, married with two young sons and has lived in Denmark since 1999.

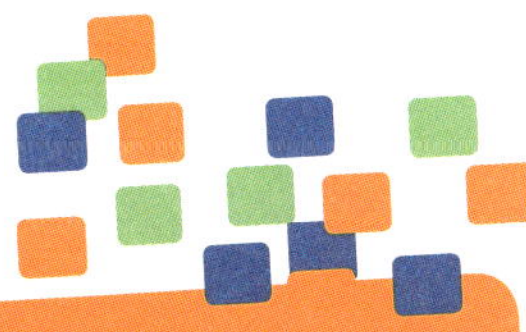

http://personprofil.aau.dk/124693#/minside

The Art of Arts Integration: *Theoretical Perspectives and Practical Guidelines*
by Tatiana Chemi
(updated and extended version of the book Kunsten at integrere kunst i undervisningen, Tatiana Chemi, Aalborg Universitetsforlag, 2012)

1. Edition

Cover: akila / Kirsten Bach Larsen
Layout: akila / Kirsten Bach Larsen

Photo on frontcover: Tatiana Chemi
Other pictures, figures and illustrations: Tatiana Chemi, 2010-2011
Photo in Figure 10: Patrick Nielsen, 2010

Printed at Toptryk Grafisk ApS, 2014
ISBN: 978-87-7112-151-3

Published by:
Aalborg University Press
Skjernvej 4A, 2nd floor
DK – 9220 Aalborg Ø
Phone: +4599407140
aauf@forlag.aau.dk
forlag.aau.dk

This book is published with financial support from Department of Learning and Philosophy, Aalborg University.